MARRIAGE AND DEATH RECORDS

ABSTRACTED FROM

THE

Newark Weekly Courier

NEW YORK

1869–1873

Harriet E. Wiles

HERITAGE BOOKS
2011

HERITAGE BOOKS
AN IMPRINT OF HERITAGE BOOKS, INC.

Books, CDs, and more—Worldwide

For our listing of thousands of titles see our website
at
www.HeritageBooks.com

A Facsimile Reprint
Published 2011 by
HERITAGE BOOKS, INC.
Publishing Division
100 Railroad Ave. #104
Westminster, Maryland 21157

Originally published in 1996
by Pipe Creek Publications

Other Heritage Books by Harriet E. Wiles:
Genealogical Abstracts from Palmyra, Wayne County, New York Newspapers, 1810-1854
S. D. Van Alstine and Harriet Wiles

— Publisher's Notice —
In reprints such as this, it is often not possible to remove blemishes from the original. We feel the contents of this book warrant its reissue despite these blemishes and hope you will agree and read it with pleasure.

International Standard Book Numbers
Paperbound: 978-1-58549-828-4
Clothbound: 978-0-7884-8806-1

INTRODUCTION

Harriet (Evretts) Wiles, the compiler of this short work, as well as others, was born in Newark, NY, the county seat of Wayne County, April 20, 1876, which explains her interest in the county and her devotion to the genealogical background of the area.

As Harriet Mae Evretts, she attended "Teachers Training School", an institution peculiar to New York State: a one year course, giving one license to teach grades one through eight for a period of three years. She also attended Columbia College [now Columbia University].

On November 7, 1898, she married Frank Burr Wiles, a native of Syracuse, NY. They made their home on East 43rd Street, New York City where she became active in the New York Genealogical & Biographical Society. She also maintained an active interest in Columbia County, NY, where she chaired the Genealogy Committee of the Columbia County Historical Society.

This work, although somewhat brief, helps fill the great void that exists in a state that did not require registration of vital records until about 1900.

The reader should be aware that this transcription of Mrs. Wiles work was made from a xerox copy of a carbon copy of the original. The latter contained numerous "strike overs" which in some instances were illegible. In such cases the transcriber has added a different possible reading of the record in parantheses. Such entries as well as others may be checked in the original issues of the newspaper, files of which can be located by inquiry to the New York State library in Albany, New York.

Mary K. Meyer
Editor

MARRIAGE AND DEATH RECORDS

Abstracted from the Newark Weekly Courier, published at Newark, NY each Thursday beginning January 14, 1869. J. L. Earll, Editor and Proprietor. (Harriet M. Wiles)

January 14, 1869
A small child of George Wright. d. Jan. 10th.

Died: Solon Taylor. (no date given).

Died: J. H. Sweeny died last week in Palmyra.

January 21, 1869
Married: in Newark, Thursday evening, Jan. 14th, in the Christian Chapel, by Rev. Mr. Burgdorf, Mr. Simeon Wicks of Phelps, Ontario Co., and Miss Catharine Shumway of Marion, Wayne Co., NY.

Married: in Newark, Dec. 31st by Rev. J. C. Burgdorf, Mr. John Case of Columbus, OH to Miss Lottie Vosburg of Newark.

January 28, 1869
Married: in Arcadia, Jan. 21, 1869, by Rev. J. C. Burgdorf, Mr. Henry Shulte to Mrs Judida Coane, both of Arcadia.

February 4, 1869
Married: in Newark, Dec. 25, at the M. E. Church by Rev. Dr. Buck, Mr. E.B.S. Landon to Miss M. Louise Crommett.

February 11, 1869
Married: at the residence of the bride's father, Dec. 24, 1868, by Rev. John Spinks, Mr. Erasmus H. Higgins, of Newark to Miss Frances Stever of Fairville.

Married: by the same [as above], at the residence of the bride's father, Jan. 26, 1869, Mr. Arthur D. Feller to Miss Catherine Wakeman, both of Arcadia.

Married: at the residence of the bride's uncle, Jan. 30, 1869, by Rev. David Croft, Mr. Charles R. St. John of Phelps, NY to Miss Carrie Hicks of Wyalusing, Bradford Co., PA.

February 18, 1860
Died: on Dec. 23rd, 1868 (sic) Mariette Galusha,

wife of J. Yates Bennett of Portage, ae 33 yrs. 19 days.
[Date should undoubtedly be 1859.]

February 25, 1860
Married: at the Methodist Church in Newark, Feb. 23, 1869, by Rev. D. D. Buck, Charles Frear to Miss Cornelia Bradt, of Iona MI.

March 4, 1869
Died: at Sodus, Aaron Clark, at the residence of his nephew, Prof. L. H. Clark, ae 69 yrs.

March 18, 1869
Married: in Arcadia , Feb. 24, 1869 by Rev. D. D. Buck, Ward Wolf and Miss Charlotte Van Gorder, both of Arcadia.

Married: by the same, at the parsonage, March 10, Levi
    A. Loveland of Newark to Miss Tryphena H. Bellows
    of Florence, NY.

Married: in Arcadia at the residence of the bride's
    father, on the 11th inst., by Rev. J. W. Spoor,
    Emsley C. Sunderlin of Chicago, IL, to Miss Ella
    Spoor of Arcadia.

March 13, 1869
Married: in Arcadia, Feb. 24, by Rev. D. D. Buck, D. D., Mr. Ward Wolff to Miss Charlotte Van Gorder, both of Arcadia.

Married: by the same, March 10, at the parsonage, Mr.
    Levi A. Loveland of Newark to Miss Tryphena H.
    Bellows of Florence, NY.

Married: in Arcadia at the residence of the bride's
    father on the 11th inst., by Rev. J. W. Spoor, Mr.
    Emsley C. Sunderlin of Chicago, IL to Miss Ella
    Spoor of Arcadia.

March 18, 1869
Died: in Sodus, March 11, Herman Deright, ae 40 years.

Died: in Sodus, March 11, Almira, wife of Morris Arms,
    ae 65 years.

Died: in Sodus, March 10th, wife of the late Orville
    Chitenden, ae 70 years

March 25, 1869
    Married: at East Newark, March 17, by Rev. B. L. Van Buren, Dwight A. Pease to Mrs. Mary French.

Married: in East Newark, March 17 (?), by Rev. J. C. Burgdorf, Mr. Melvin Meachem of Grinnell, IA and Miss Emma J. Ottman of Newark, NY.

Died: at Fort Plain, NY, Nettie Mayer, wife of John Tingue. [A later issue says she d. in New York city, March 10th in the 25th yr. of her age. She was the dau. of H. F. C. and Eve A. Mayer of Newark. Burial in Fort Plain.]

April 8, 1869
    Died: at Sodus, March 28th, Samuel Felshaw, ae 68 years.

Died: at Sodus, March 30th, S. P. Johnson, formerly proprietor of the <u>Johnson House</u> at Sodus Point, ae 57 yrs. His wife d. April 3rd, ae 56 years.

April 22, 1869
    Married: in Sodus on the 15th inst., at the residence of J. Gramke, Esq., Mr. Henry Beiler of Pultneyville, and Miss Mary Gramke.

Died: at Sodus, April 16, James Hopkins, ae 68 yrs.

Died: at Sodus, April 18th, Mrs. J. G. Kelley, ae 64 yrs.

April 29, 1869
    Married: at Newark, April 22, by Rev. G. R. Pierce, Mr. James Austin of Rochester, and Miss Rhoda Smith of Newark.

Married: at Sodus, April 25th at the residence of the bride's father, by Rev. J. Ireland, Dr. Eggleston of Marshall, MI and Emma, dau. of C. R. Borrodaile, Esquire.

May 6, 1869
    Married: in Sodus, at the residence of the bride's father, on May 3rd, William Swales and Mary, dau. of L. Whitney, Esq.

Married: in Butler on May 4th by Rev. Mr. Abbott, Mr. J. H. Dowd of Newark to Miss Cassie Cole of Butler.

May 13, 1869
    Married: at Newark, May 5th, by Rev J. C. Burgdurf,

Mr. E. L. Hodskin of Fairport, [Monroe Co.] and Miss Libbie A. Butler of Newark.

Married: at the Methodist Church, May 11th, by Rev.D. D. Buck, D.D., Mr. S. Porter Hough of Detroit, MI to Miss Kittie A. Runyon of Newark.

June 3, 1869
Married: at the residence of Rev. L. W. Cronk, in Arcadia, May 19th by Rev. J. Spinks of Fairville, Mr. Philetus M. Skuse to Miss Ida B. Cronk, both of Arcadia.

Married: in Newark, at the residence of Dr. Parker, May 27th, by Rev. D. D. Buck, D.D., Mr. William H. Keller to Miss Harriet L. Aldrich.

June 17, 1869
Died: at Sodus, June 8, 1869, L. Sanford Allen, ae 62 years.

July 1, 1869
Married: on June 23rd, at the residence of the bride's father, in Arcadia, by Rev. W. W. Runyan, Mr. Albert Amerman of New York City and Miss Alethia Estelle, only dau. of Norman Culver.

Died: at Hillsdale, MI , June 28th, Belcher, eldest son of our former townsman, Horace Blackmar.

July 22, 1869
Died: Mr. John Daggett of California..absent from Newark 17 years.

August 19, 1869
Married: at the Christian Church in Newark, Aug. 17th, by Rev. J. C. Burgdorf, Mr. Benson C. Drake to Miss Mary C. Drake, of Newark.

August 26, 1869
Died: last week, Milton S. Brown, in Newark.

Died: Aug. 5th, in Newark, Melzer N. Aldrich, son of Myron H., and Rebecca B. Aldrich, ae 16 years.

September 9, 1869
Married: at the residence of Mr. A. Horn, in Phelps by Rev. G. Van Alstyne, Mr. Daniel E. Taylor to Miss Anna M. Davison, both of Phelps.

Married: in Newark, Sept. 1st, by Rev. J. C. Burgdorf, Mr. Sylvester Van Vrocklin, of Rome, NY, to Miss Emma Haight of Newark.

Died: in Newark, Miss Betsey Webster in her 72nd yr.

Died: Aug. 28th, Nancy, widow of the late William Gaylord of Kansas, ae 57 years.

Died: at Newark, Sept. 9th, William Harding in his 22nd year.

Died: in Dundee, Monroe Co., MI Aug. 28th, Mr. Isaac Stephenson, ae 71 yrs. For 20 yrs., Mr. S. was a resident of Arcadia, NY.

September 16, 1869
    Married: in Newark, Sept. 10th, by Rev.J.C. Burgdorf, Mr. George Hicks of Phelps to Miss Emma G. Bell of Clifton.

Killed: near Grand Rapids, MI, H. H. Wallace, son of Mr. Samuel Wallace of Newark, ae 24 yrs.

September 23, 1869
    Married: in Newark, Sept. 22, by Rev. J. C. Burgdorf, Mr. John S. Krum to Miss Adella O. Krum, all of Newark.

The following deaths occurred in Sodus:
    Libbie Gothorpe, ae 28 years.
    Freelove, wife of Jacob Pitcher, ae 58 years.
    Mrs. Amy Williams, age 80 yrs. - her husband, Joseph d. 11 yrs.ago; resident of Sodus 50 years.
    Mrs.G. H. Mason d. Sept. 24th, ae 43 years.

September 30, 1869
    Married: at Orleans, Ontario Co., NY, June 27th, by Rev. J. A. Wader, Mr. R. Almon Lusk of Manchester to Miss Minnie Lusk of Newark. Married: at Hope Chapel in Newark, Sept. 22nd, by Rev.Mr. Pettengill of Palmyra, Mr. William S. Bryant of Manchester to Miss Ella D. Lusk of Newark.

Married: at the residence of the bride's father, Sept. 22nd, by Rev. W.A. McCorkle, Mr. Frank Blackmar of Hillsdale, MI (formerly of Newark) to Miss Jessie R. McCollum of Detroit, MI.

Married: at the Methodist Church, Sept. 30th, by Rev. Walton W. Batershall, of Rochester, Mr. Ludlow B. Ward to Miss Ella Cronise, both of Newark, NY.

Married: At the same time and place [as above] Mr. George B. Taylor and Miss Eustatia Ward of Newark.

October 7, 1869
Married: in Fairville, Oct. 6th, by Rev. J. Spinks, at the residence of the bride's father, Mr. Michael Wickman to Miss Ann Amelia Sayles (sister of Manley), all of Arcadia.

October 14, 1869
Died: in Geneva, NY, Oct. 12th, Mrs. Philena Buck, wife of Rev. D. D. Buck, ae 52 yrs.; bur. in Mt. Hope Cemetery.

Died: Oct. 5th, at Sodus, Betsey, wife of Andrew Wilbur, ae 52 years.

Died: in Newark, Oct. 9th, Mable, only dau. of Nathan and Eliza Knapp, ae 1-5-18.

October 21, 1869
Married: Oct.14th, by Rev. Mr. Randolph, Mr. John J. Cornwall of Battle Creek, MI to Miss Ellen M., dau. of Carles [sic] [Charles?] Stebbins of Arcadia.

Married: in Newark, Oct. 18, 1869 by Rev. J. C. B Burgdorf, Mr. William Burleigh of Arcadia to Miss Eva Ridley of Newark.

Died: in Arcadia, Oct. 13th, Mrs. Hannah Cole, in her 51st year.

Died: in Sodus, Oct.16th, Mrs. Morris Decay, ae 63 years.

Married: in Newark, Oct. 14, 1869, by Rev. M. Randolph, Mr. Murray Colwell to Miss Libbie Rockfeller, both of Clifton.

October 28, 1869
Married: at the home of the bride's father, Oct. 27th, by Rev. George VanAlstyne, Mr. Orrin Danford of Sodus to Miss Frank W. Chapman of Newark.

Married: at Shortsville, Oct. 5, by Rev. L. R. Janes, Mr. William M. DeGraff of Newark to Miss Emma Van Duzen of Geneva.

Married: at the parsonage in Fairville, by Rev. J. Spinks, Oct. 3, Mr. Isaac Wilson to Miss Harriet Celia Onderkonk, both of Sodus.

November 11, 1869
Died: Mr. Elias North of Savannah.

Died: in Providence, RI, Nov. 14th, Samuel C. Garlock, son of George and Matilda Garlock, ae 19-11-19. Buried in Newark.

November 25, 1859
Married: by G.R.H. Shumway, at the residence of the bride's father, Baron A. Meade to Miss Nellie M. Foster.

December 2, 1869
Married: in Newark, by Rev. W. Piggot, Henry T. Williams of Camden, to Miss Louisa Krum of Newark.

Married: at Newark in the Presbyterian church on Thursday, Nov. 25, by Rev. A. H. Lilly, William E. Post of East Palmyra, and Emma Maria VanInwagen of Arcadia.

Married: at East Palmyra, Nov. 24th by Rev. A. H. Lilly, Samuel Albert Sherman and Jeanette Kelsey, all of East Palmyra.

Died: in Sodus, Nov. 23rd, Madison L. Stearns, ae 49 years.

December 9, 1869
Married: by Rev. Isaac Gibbard, Dec. 1st, Mr. Francis J. Lord, son of Ichabod Lord, Esq. of Phelps to Miss Anna P. St. John, dau of Charles G. St. John, of Newark, NY.

Married: in Newark, by Rev. J. D. Burgdorf, Dec. 2nd, Mr. Daniel L. Hartman to Miss Sally N. Neiderlander.

Died: Mr. Allyn, a miserly man worth $600,000, d. lately leaving property to 17 heirs. His executors were his sister, Mrs. Susan Allyn Brown, and his brothers, Capt. Christopher Allyn of Ledyard, and Mr. Henry Allyn of Palmyra, NY.

Died: last week, Mr. Ridley, a resident of Phelps for 56 years.

Died: in East Newark, Dec. 1st, Mr. Elihu Ridley, ae 59 years.

December 16, 1869
Married: On Dec. 15th, by Rev. J. T. Steeley of Clifton, NY, Mr. John L. Smith to Miss Lena Short, both of Port Gibson.

Died: in Newark, Dec. 5th, Mrs. Sarah Rowe, in her 78th year.

Died: at Pattens Mill near Waco, TX, Sept. 20, 1861, James W. Patten, formerly of Newark, ae 67-9-28. At the same place, Oct.13, 1869. Died: at the same place, Oct. 16th, Julius C. Patten, ae 42-2-13; also at the same place, Mrs. Narcissa Patten, ae 68-5-28.

Died: at the residence of her son, Jesse B. Odell, Dec. 11th, Susan Odell, ae 87-6-0.

December 23, 1869
Married: in Arcadia, at the residence of Norman Culver on Dec. 16th, by Rev. A. H. Lilly, Albert G. McFarland of Chagrin Falls, OH to Christina Littebrant of Arcadia.

January 6, 1870
Married: in Newark, Jan. 5th, by Rev. G. Van Alstyne, Allyn B. Billings of Macedon to Miss Alma Barhite of Newark.

January 20, 1870
Married: in Newark, Jan. 1st, by Rev. J. C. Burgdorf, Mr. Harry Drake to Miss Mary E. Munford.

January 27, 1870
Died: on Dec. 23rd, at the residence of his son, Dr. R. Thomas in Newark, Rodman Thomas, ae 84 yrs. He was b. May 1, 1785 in Berlin, Rensselear Co., NY, youngest of 12 children - 6 sons and 6 daus. The family removed from RI to Rensselear Co.; the oldest brother was in the Revolution and died at 26 yrs. Rodman has 3 children; his wife d. in July 1838. He came with his son, Dr. Thomas to Newark in 1857.

February 3, 1870
Died: in Newark, Jan. 27th, William Sturgess, ae 65 years.

February 10, 1870
Died: at Sodus, Feb. 3rd, John Mesick, ae 24 years.

February 17, 1870
Married: in Rochester, Feb. 9, 1870, by Rev. A. H. Lilly, Milton C. Jagger of East Palmyra and Pamela Button, eldest dau. of Alexandria Button of Greece, NY.

Married: Sodus, Miss Frank Case, eldest surviving dau. of Gamaliel Case to William B. Morse of Rochester, by her brother, pastor of the M.E. Church of Elmira.

Died: in Sodus, Feb. 12th, Jeremiah Hughson, ae 69 years.

Died: in Sodus, Feb. 13th, John Dodd, ae 80 years.

February 24, 1870
Died: in Newark, Feb. 19th, George A., son of John R. and Mary A. Westfall, ae 7-8-0.

Died: at Sodus, Marion, dau. of S. P.Hulett, Feb. 14th, ae 9 months.

March 3, 1870
Married: in Newark, Feb. 25th, by Rev. J. C. Burgdorf, James Harding of Arcadia, to Jennie Harmon of Phelps.

March 10, 1870
Sodus items:
Died: Feb. 28, 1870, George Seargeant. age 78 yrs.; resident of Sodus for 60 years.
Died: Feb. 27th, Matthew Pettys, ae 68 years.
Died: Feb. 27th, Florence, dau. of William Champlin, ae 11 years.
Died: Mar. 5th, Francis A., son of Thomas Padget, ae 4 months.

Died: in Newark, Mar. 4th, W. O. Sherman, ae 49 yrs.; came here in 1854; living with his older brother, D. A. Sherman. He left a widow.

March 24, 1870
Married: by Rev. Mr. Rudd, as the residence of the bride's parents in Newark, last Thurs., Hon. T. W. Collins, late County Clerk and Miss Cornie E. Bottum, dau. of Dr. B. W. Bottum.

Married: at Sodus, Andrew J. Brown to Laura Weet, March 10th, by Rev. Mr. Miles.

Died: in Jackson, MI, Victor M. Bostwick, formerly a resident here but for 11 yrs. a citizen of Jackson, MI. Leaves a wife and 6 children.

Died: Mar. 20th, Allen Goodsell, ae 27 yrs.; leaves a wife and child (or children?)

March 31, 1870
Married: at Sodus March 23rd, Frank Collins and Miss Hattie Williams, dau. of Charles Williams, Esq., both of Sodus.

April 7, 1870
Died: in Sodus last Wed., Freeman Ostrander, a Union soldier, formerly of Dutchess Co., NY; lived with Rowland Robinson.

Died: in Sodus, Miss D. J. Sabine, ae 18 yrs.

Died: in Sodus, Apr. 2nd, Jennie, dau. of James DeBrine, ae 2 years.

Died: Leander S. Ketchum of Clyde. [No age given]

Died: last week, Mr. Cullen Foster, ae 69 yrs.; resident of Lyons, ae 40 years.

April 14, 1870
Married: at Sodus, by Rev. E. P. Smith, Thomas Cartman to Lydia Boyer, on Apr. 10th.

Married: at the residence of the bride's father, on Apr. 6th, by Rev. S. Krum, Mr. Jacob L. Snyder to Miss Eliza J. Beckwith, both of Arcadia.

April 21, 1870
Married: Apr. 19th, by J.A.H. Cornell, D.D., Mr. E. W. Weeks to Miss Lucia H. Lay, dau. of Robert S. Lay, Esq., of Newark.

Died: at his residence in Cherry Valley, Otsego Co., NY, Judge James S. Campbell, ae 91 yrs.

Died: in Sodus, George, son of John Swales, ae 1 year.

Died: in Sodus, Apr. 16th, Martin Garrison, ae 80 years.

April 28, 1870
Married: in Fairville, March 13th, by Rev. John Spink, Mr. James P. Austin to Miss Mary DeVolder, both of Arcadia.

Married: by Rev. John Spink, April 20th, Mr. Louis Laubenheimer of Joy, to Miss Anna M. Willworth of Liverpool, NY.

Married: by Rev. John Spink, April 24th, Mr. Myron E. Clark to Miss Adeliza Tyler, both of Arcadia.

Died: near South Sodus, Jonathan Butler, ae 72 years.

Died: Apr. 22nd, Elias R. Agans, ae 72 years.

May 5, 1870
    Married: in East Newark, by Rev. J. C. Burgdorf, Mr. Edward H. Babcock of Port Gibson to Miss Ellen Hanson of Palmyra.

m. in Sodus, April 26, 1870, by Rev. John Dyson, Mr. Alonzo H. King of Oneida, NY to Miss Francisca G. Odell of Sodus.

Sodus items:
    Died: Apr. 26, Jane, wife of Clark Reynold of Lyons, ae 48 yrs.

    Died: Apr. 25th, Jane, dau. of William Pierce of Williamson, ae 24 yrs.

    Died: May 1st, Sarah, relict of the late John Buerman, ae 77 years.

May 19, 1870
    Married: in Newark at the Universalist Church, May 18th, by Rev. George W. Montgomery, Mr. George Z. T. Kenyon of Odell, IL to Miss Nettie A. Maine of Newark.

Died: in Newark, May 5th, Nellie Frear, ae 6-2-17.

May 26, 1870
    Died: in Arcadia, May 15th, Byron R., son of J. P. and Abigail Welcher, ae 15-5-15.

June 30, 1870
    Married: on June 16th, at Grace Church in Lyons, NY, by Rev. W. H. Williams, J. C. Robinson of New York to Miss Fanny M. Cramer, only dau. of George W. Cramer, Esq. of Lyons.

July 7, 1870
    Married: in Newark, July 2nd, by Rev. J. C. Burgdorf, Mr. Edwin R. Brower of Phelps to Miss Alice Johnson of Newark.

    Married: in Newark, June 30, by Rev. R. Dunning, Mr. Charles Bennett, of Williamson, NY to Miss Phebe Jane Bishop of Ontario, NY.

July 14, 1870
    Married: in Taunton, MA, July 5th by Rev. Dr. Pollard, Mr. William H. Nicholoy (s) of Newark to Miss Alice B. Eddy of Taunton, MA.

Married: in Sturgis, MI, July 5th, by Rev. W. J. Spaulding, Mr. Frank H. Stroud of Eaton Rapids, MI, to Miss Ludelia Evans of Newark, NY.

Married: on July 5th, Henry Dodd to Emma Seymour.

Died: in Newark, July 8th, Mary, wife of Oliver Crothers, ae 24 years.

Died: in Sodus: d. July 9th, Mrs. Isaac Davidson, ae 70 years.

July 21, 1870
Died: in Sodus: d. July 9th, Nathan R. Strong, ae 69 years.

Died: Miss Eliza Wilcox, ae 64 years.

Died: Phebe, wife of C. A. Saddler, ae 45 years.

August 4, 1870
Died: in Sodus: d. July 23, Elizabeth, wife of Charles Arms, ae 45 years.

Died: July 29th, Sally, wife of the late Benaga Gibbs, ae 74 years.

August 11, 1870
Married: July 27th, Dwight A. Bolster of Coldwater, MI to Miss Flora D. Vanderhoof, at the residence of the bride's brother, Allen Vanderhoof of Coldwater, MI. by Rev. E. Cooley.

August 18, 1870
Died: in Arcadia, Aug. 9th, Mrs. Martha Barton, wife of Elihu Barton, ae 50-2-25.

August 25, 1870
Died: in Sodus, Aug. 11th, Elmore, son of John Wood, ae 6 years.

Died: Aug. 8th, Miss Almyra Smith, ae 55 years.

September 15, 1870
Married: at Sodus, Sept. 3rd, F. A. Bolls to Mrs. Wealthy Delevan, by Rector E. P. Smith.

Married: in Arcadia at the residence of the bride's father, by Rev. Richard Dunning, Dr. J. B. McLean of St. Johns. MI to Miss Vietta V. Bryant of Arcadia.

Died: in Sodus: d. 6 Sept., Fanny, relict of the late Jerry Cady, ae 79 years.

Died: in Sodus, Sept. 12th, infant son of Charles Mills, ae 3 months.

Died: Aug. 6th, in Sturgis, MI, Dora Belle Evans, ae 1-7-11 and on Aug. 11th, Hattie May Evans, ae 8 yrs., daus. of Monroe and Cornelia M. Evans, formerly of Newark.

Died: in Williamson, Sept. 5th, Mrs. Sarah Reeves, ae 91 yrs., one of the earliest settlers of the Town of Palmyra in 1799, Her husband was Paul Reeves who built the first mill on Mud Creek. She was the mother of James Reeves of Newark.

Died: at Pultneyville, Sept. 3rd, Zimri Waters, in his 59th year.

September 22, 1870
Married: Sept. 15th, John Royce of Pultneyville to Mary, dau. of Robert Fellers of Sodus by Rev. T. Ireland.

Died: Sept. 16th, Nancy, wife of the late Jeduthan Moffit, ae 89 yrs.. In the spring of 1794, at age 12 yrs. with her parents and grandmother, she moved to the wilds of Sodus from the State of MA. Her grandmother d. at the age of 100; the mother, Mrs. Olcox, d. at 85; the father d. about 1860. She herself, had no children.

September 29, 1870
Died: in Sodus, Sept. 22nd, John Sours, ae 66 years.

Died: in Sodus, Sept. 25th, Charles, son of Abram VanAuken, ae 16 years.

October 6, 1870
Died: in Newark, Oct. 1st, Albert A. Bryant, ae 35 years.

Died: Sept. 29th, at the residence of his son-in-law, Mr. Thomas Percy, Mr.Martin Lanridge, ae 81 yrs.

Oct. 13, 1870
Married: Oct. 5th, by Rev. J. Pierce, Mr. Judson Fisk to Miss Alice Hunt.

Married: Oct. 11th by Rev. G. R. Pierce, Mr. Frank Yeo and Miss Kate Hill.

Married: Oct. 2nd, by Rev. George VanAlstyne, Mr. Frederick Gauthner, Jr. to Miss Christine Diets, both of Lyons.

Married: Oct 12th, by Rev. George Van Alstyne, Mr. Samuel S. Reynolds, to Miss Eliza Palmeter of Phelps.

Married: Oct. 12th, by Rev. George Van Alstyne, Mr. Cyrus A. Tater to Miss Mary J. Burgess, both of Phelps.

Died: at Sodus, Oct. 7th, George W. Paddock, ae 59 yrs. He came to Sodus in 1811 from Rensselear Co., NY.

Died: Oct. 4th, Thomas Robinson, ae 80 yrs. He came from England in 1817 and settled in Sodus.

October 27, 1870
Died: at Sodus, Oct. 18th, Samuel Davenport, ae 68 years.

Died: d. on Oct. 20th, Helen, Wife of B. Garret and dau. of H. Barclay ae 20 years.

Died: Oct. 22nd, Manle [sic] Gibbs, ae 17 yrs; left a twin brother, Martin.

November 3, 1870
Married: at the residence of Chester F. Short in Newark, by Elder J. Chapman, on Nov. 1st, Mr. Thomas Kesson of Albany to Miss Sarah E. Fonda of Gorham, NY.

Married: at Hooper's Hotel at East Newark, Oct. 22nd, by J. L. Hadden, Esq., Mr. Milo S. White to Miss Hattie Sutton, both of Williamson, NY.

November 10, 1870
Died: Nov. 1st, at Sodus Point, Mrs. William Buys, ae 44 years.

Died: at Sodus, Nov. 1st, Mrs. William Buys, ae 44 years.

November 17, 1870
Married: at the bride's residence in Phelps, by Rev. J. C. Burgdorf, Mr. S. L. Olmstead of Arcadia to Miss Dollie Harman.

Died: in Sodus, Nov. 11th, Jennie, dau. of A. Kennedy, ae 4 years.

November 24, 1870
Married: Nov. 22nd in St. John's Church, Buffalo, NY, by Rt. Rev. A. C. Cox, Bishop of western NY, Joel Henry Prescott and Miss Helen J. Harding, all of Buffalo.

Died: at Sodus on Nov. 11th, Mary, wife of the late Thomas Martin and sister of B. F. Norris, Esq., ae 53 years.

December 1, 1870
Married: in Newark, Nov. 23rd, by Rev. G. R. Pierce, Mr. Pliny Hill of Decatur, IL, to Miss Susie Hill of Newark.

December 9, 1870
Married: at the bride's residence in Phelps, Nov. 30th, by Rev. J. C. Burgdorf, Mr. Wilson A. Langdon of Lyons to Miss Lurinda L. Hornbeck of Phelps.

December 16, 1870
Married: in Arcadia, Dec. 13th, by Rev. George Van Alstyne, Mr. Aaron D. Lamoreaux to Miss Estelle M. Cronise.

December 23, 1870
Married: at the residence of the bride's father, Dec. 15th, by Rev. Edward Ingersoll, D. D., Stephen Fish Sherman and Agnes R., dau. of Charles G. Irish of Buffalo.

Married: Nov 22nd, in St. John's Church in Buffalo, by Rt. Rev. A. C. Cox, Bishop of Western New York, Joel Henry Prescott to Miss Helen J. Harding of Buffalo, NY.

Died: Dec. 15th, at Joy, Mrs. John Pulver, ae 36 years.

Married: at the bride's residence, Dec. 20th, by Rev. J.C. Burgdorf, Mr. James Tonsworth to Miss M. E. Roberts, both of Phelps.

December 30, 1870
Married: in Newark, Dec. 27th, by Rev. J. C. Burgdorf, Dr. A. R. Freeman, of Westboro, MA, to Miss M. E. Parks, of Newark.

January 6, 1871
Married: in Newark, Dec. 27th, by Rev. Mr. Sewell, Mr. Gardner M. Soverhill of Bradford, IL to Miss Josie Willett, of Newark, NY.

January 12, 1871
Married: at South Easton, NY, by Rev. G. P. Sewall of Cayuga, Rev. A. C. Sewall, Pastor of the Presbyterian Church of Newark to Miss Helen S. Ives of South Easton.

Died: Jan. 9th, Mrs. Hannah H. Kelley, wife of C. P. Kelley, of Phelps, ae 40 yrs.

January 23, 1871
Died: at Sodus, Jan. 8th, Mrs. Joseph Tenley, ae 68 years.

Died: Jan. 13th, Emily, wife of George Kelley, ae 30 years.

Died: Jan. 12th, at Pultneyville, Asahel Todd, M. D., ae 84 years.

January 26, 1871 [date of this edition may be an error]:
Died: in Brooklyn, Jan. 16th, Carrrie C., only child of Charles R. and Carrie M. Adams, ae 4 yrs., 6 mos. Buried in Albany.

Died: in Newark, Jan. 18th, Caroline, wife of Albert E. Jackson, ae 59 yrs, 9 months.

February 9, 1871
Married: at the Black Bear Quartz Mining Company's Works, Klamath Co. (OR?), Dec. 17th, by Hon. John T. Carey, Hon, John Daggett, formerly of Newark, to Miss Alice P. Foree.

Died: at Newark, Jan. 30th, James T. Bryant, ae 70 yrs., b. in Morris Co., NJ Sept. 6, 1801, migrated to Cayuga Co., in 1803, and in 1806 came to Newark.

February 23, 1871
Died: last Tues., Calvin King of Phelps.

Died: in Arcadia, Feb. 9th, at the residence of her son, Benjamin Bailey, Mrs. Evangelia Bailey, ae 85-9-0.

March 2, 1871
Died: at Newark, Feb. 22nd, Z. W. Smith, ae 57 years.

Died: at Sodus Center, Mr. James Hodge, ae 84 yrs. A pioneer.

Died: in Palmyra, Mrs. David P. Sanford.

March 16 1871
Died: March 12th, Elizabeth Tillotson of Morenci, MI, formerly of Newark, ae 65 years.

March 23, 1871
Died: March 21st, in Phelps, Dr. Joel Prescott, ae 86 yrs 8 mos. 2 days. He was the father of Joel H. Prescott of Newark and one of the early settlers of Phelps in 1807...[lived] there 64 years.

Died: in Lyons, March 16th, Miss Eliza Bradley, sister of Benjamin J. Bradley and Mrs. Nelson Hazen, ae 52 years.

Died: in Sodus, March 15th, Mr. Moses Neale, ae 30 yrs. Came from England 14 years ago; lived until 20 mos. ago in Phelps.

Died: in Sodus, March 19th, Emma, dau. of William Tryon, ae 34 years.

March 30, 1871
Item from the **Phelps Citizen**: Dr. Joel Prescott came from Westford, MA in 1807, studied medicine with his uncle, Dr. Joel Prescott who d. in 1811.

April 6, 1871
Waterloo item: Benjamin Horton was killed by Frances Barnard.

April 13, 1871
Died: in Palmyra, Lemuel Durfee.

May 4, 1871
Married: Mr. Dewitt Westfall to Miss Louise Jeremiah

Died: in Lyons, Mr. Baltzell.

Died: in Lyons, Walter Van Duesen, ae about 70 yrs.

May 11, 1871
Died: in Sodus, J. Birdsall.

May 18, 1871
Married: May 9, by Rev. S. H. Mirrick, Nathaniel Freeman of Lawrence, SC to Miss Dell A. Higgins of Leroy, New York.

May 25, 1871
   Married: in Newark, May 23rd, by Rev. A C. Sewall, Byron Thomas to Miss Nellie C. Smith.

June 8, 1871
   Married: June 27th by Rev. R. Hogoboom, John Stuart to Sarah E. Reed, both of Newark.

Died: at Williamson, June 1st, Mrs. Joshua Baker, ae 67 years.

Died: in Hartford, CT, recently, John Knox, ae 40 yrs. - from near Palmyra.

July 13, 1871
   Died: in Newark, June 29th, Ella Todd, wife of John Dillenback, ae 24 yrs. 2 days.

Died: July 8th, Mrs. John N. Brownell, wife of the Sheriff. She was the only dau. of Richard Button, of Williamson.

July 20, 1871
   Died: last Wed., at Manchester, Hugh S. Mosher, ae 80 years.

Married: at Ontario, July 3rd, a dau. of Col. Joseph W. Corning to Mr. Charles Wilbur.

July 27, 1871
   Died: last Tuesday, at Marion, Charles Cory, an elderly man.

August 3, 1871
   Died: in Newark, July 26th, William C. Mills, ae 63 years.

August 24, 1871
   Died: at Red Creek, Aug. 2nd, Dr. Campbell. He graduated at Geneva, NY [Hobart?] in 1832; commenced practice in South Butler, remaining until 1854 when he removed to Battle Creek, MI. In 1858 he removed to Atchinson, Kansas, then in 1862 went into the Army as a Surgeon. At the close of the war in 1865, he went to Savannah [NY or GA?]. In 1870 came to Red Creek.

September 7, 1871
   Married: in Clyde, by Rev. A. A. Thayer of New York City, John E. McGinnis to Emma Brown, both of Clyde.

Died: in Palmyra, Hattie L. Barnhart, ae 7 mos. 6 days.

Died: in Palmyra, Mrs. Louisa Fahnstock, ae 28 yrs. (Monroe , MI papers please copy.)

Died: in Lyons, Aug. 30th, Frances Male, ae 66-3-1.

Died: in Williamson, Aug. 26th, Mrs. Ann Pierce, widow of William Pierce, age 72 years.

September 14, 1871
Married: at Honeoye Falls, NY, Sept. 12th, by Rev. S. Alden Freeman, Charles H. Jameson of Newark to Emma C. Allen.

Married: recently, Alice J., dau. of Dr. J. H. Stafford of Canajoharie, NY. [No bridegroom mentioned.]

Died: in Galen, Aug. 25th, Harvey Wilson Reed, son of Charles H. and Sarah A. Reed, ae 6 years.

Died: in Walrath, Aug. 29th, Phebe Grandin, widow of William L. Grandin, in her 73rd year.

Died: in Walworth, Aug. 20th, Riley Hill, ae 66 years.

Died: W. Gibbs, ae 40 yrs.; leaves four children, the youngest of which is 2 months.

Died: Sept. 10th, Myron, son of Josiah Rice, ae 27 yrs.

Died: Sept. 10th, Lucia, wife of Jacob Pulver, ae 34 yrs., leaves two children..

Died: in Palmyra, Sept. 12th, at the home of her father, William L. Tucker, Helen M., wife of George A. Culver, of Annapolis, MD, in her 29th year..

September 21, 1871
Married: in Cazenovia, [Madison Co., NY], Sept. 7, at the residence of the bride's brother, by Rev. A. P. Smith, D. D., Willard N. Field of Clyde, to Miss Lucy N. Forte of Cazenovia.

Married: in Palmyra, Sept. 11th, Mr. Charles H. Clarke, NY to Miss Helen A. Bump of Manchester, NY.

Married: in Mendon, NY, Sept. 14th, by Rev.J. D. Smith, James Stark to Miss Martha Jane Bennett, both of Williamson.

Died: in Lyons, Sept. 7th, Lucius Cole, ae 83 years.

Died: in Lebanon, [Madison Co.], NY, Aug. 29th, Mrs. Sophia Reed, wife of E. D. Reed, ae 63 yrs.

Died: in Clayville, Oneida Co., NY, Sept. 4th, Mrs. Eliza McMannus Martin, wife of Hiram Martin, formerly a resident of Newark.

September 28, 1871
    Married: Sept. 20th, by Rev. J. W. Burgdorf, Charles E. Marsh of Evansville, IN, to Miss Emma E. Husted of Arcadia.

Married: Sept. 16th, Stephen Townsend to Susan Lucena Bennett, both of Palmyra.

Married: Sept. 20th, Daniel G. Smith of Waterford, NY to Mrs. Minerva Van Wickle of Palmyra.

Died: in Manchester, Ontario Co., NY, Sept. 5th, Electa Parker, ae 63 years.

Died: in Galen, NY, Sept. 15th, Emily L., dau. of J. G. and L. Vanderpool, and wife of A. T. Jones, ae 26 years.

Died: in Lyons, Sept. 25th, John J. Westfall, ae 34 years.

Died: in Burlington, IA, Sept. 12th, Mrs. Mary Johnson, wife of Robert N. Moore, formerly of Sodus.

Died: in Huron, Sept. 24th, Richard Harris.

Died: in Sodus. Sept. 18th, Nancy, wife of Robert Fulton, ae 57 yrs.

Died: in Sodus, Sept. 22, Ann B., wife of the late S. B. McIntyre, ae 65 yrs., She was the dau. of an early pioneer, Ammi Ellsworth, who moved to Sodus in 1801.

Died: in Sodus, Sept. 25th, the infant dau. of David Knight.

October 5, 1871:
    Married: Sept. 21st, by Rev. H. Eaton, D.D., Mr. Walter S. Newbury to Miss Ann Miller, both of Palmyra.

Married: in Fairfield, IA, Sept. 28th, by Rev. Chauncey Darby, Prof. A. C. Potter of Marion, NY to Miss Etta Howe.

Married: in Bristol, Ontario Co., NY, Sept. 27th, Mr. William Elbert Spier of Lyons, to Miss Etta Case of Bristol.

Married: in Savannah, NY, Sept. 27th, Mr. Henry H. Daboll of Jordan, (Onondaga Co., NY), to Miss Fanny Andrews of Savannah.

Died: last week, Mr. James Burnett; buried at Newark; one of our oldest citizens.

Died: in Sodus, Sept. 27th, Wandall Pulver, ae 75 years.

Died: in Sodus, Sept. 28th, Sarah, dau. of George Box, ae 21 yrs.

Died: in Sodus, Sept. 30th, John Graves, ae 45 years.

October 12, 1871
Married: Oct. 2nd, Mr. Jacob Stack to Miss Ellen Hunter, both of Clyde, NY.

Married: in Fairville, Oct. 4th, Mr. Levi Ellsworth of Sodus, NY to Miss Hannah Harden, by George E. Robinson Esq..

Married: in Lyons, Oct. 3rd, Mr. George Alonzo Newman of Phelps to Miss Mary Janet Dickinson of Lyons.

Married: in Sodus, Oct 5th, Eli Darling to Emma J. Avery.

Died: in Lyons, Oct.4th, Rebecca, wife of Peter Vandeberg, ae 46 years.

Died: in Galen, Oct. 3rd, Mr. Alex Gross, ae 58 years.

Died: in Arcadia, Oct.5th, W. Wolson, ae 83 years.

Died: in Arcadia, Oct. 7th, Lucy Reed, ae 67 years.

Died: in Sodus, Oct. 4th, Mrs. Atkinson, mother of Mrs. A. Smith, ae 82 yrs.

Died: Oct. 8th, Luke C. Johnson, ae 77 yrs.

Died: Oct. 4th, William Johnson, ae about 70 yrs.

Died: Oct. 8th, Austin Rice, ae 75 yrs.
[The three deaths above may have been in Sodus.]

October 19, 1871
Married: in Manchester, Oct 13, Mr. Howland P. Wells to Miss Nettie A. Clark.

Married: in Newark, Oct 11th, by Rev. J. C. Burgdorf, Ferdando Austin, to Effie Parks, both of Newark.

Married: in Newark, Oct. 12th, by Rev. J.C. Burgdorf, James W. West and Addie Miller, both of Newark.

ITEM: Mr. and Mrs. Baily Foster celebrated their 50th wedding anniversary on Oct 15th.

Died: on Oct. 17th, in Schenectady, Eugene Elmendorf, ae 34 years.

Died: in Charlotte, MI, Oct. 2, James N. Sanford, brother of Mrs. S. H. Skinner, age 51 yrs.

Died: in Sodus, Oct. 14th, Mrs. Burtiss Currey, ae about 35 years.

October 26, 1871
Married: in Junius, NY, Oct 18th, Henry S. Whitbeck of Lyons to Amanda Terbush.

Died: in Palmyra, Mrs. Phebe Babcock, ae 53 years.

Died: in Phelps, Oct. 15th, Mrs. J. Leach, ae 57 [67?] years.

Died: in Phelps, Oct. 17th, Julia Ann, wife of D. B. Sweet, ae 61-9-0.

Died: in Phelps, Oct. 9th, Olney Hall, ae 61-6-0.

November 2, 1871
Married: Oct 25th, at the residence of the bride's father, by Rev. Louis VanDyck of Buffalo, William P. M. Colvin and Mary Ann Munson, eldest dau. of O. T. Ladue, Esq., all of Wolcott.

Married: in Lyons, Oct. 25th, Mr. Dewitt P. Foster of Prescott, AZ and Miss M. Albertine Mirick, youngest dau., of Col. Ira Mirick, of Lyons, NY.

Married: in New Haven, CT, Oct. 18th, Mr. Joseph C. [O?] Petrie and Miss Supple, formerly of Lyons, all of New Haven.

Died: in Wolcott, Oct. 22, at the residence of her son, Dr. A. P. Crafts, Mrs. Emily A. Crafts, ae 74 yrs.

November 16, 1871
Married: at the residence of the bride's parents, near Port Gibson, Nov. 14th, by Rev. W. W. Runyon, Mr. George E. Bockover to Miss Emma J. Post, dau. of Henry Post.

Married: Nov. 8th, Andrew B. Jones of Albany to Miss Alice Tucker, youngest dau. of Pomeroy Tucker, Esq.

Married: at the National Hotel, in Auburn, NY, Nov. 8th, by Rev. J. H. Harter, Revilo M. See, of Arcadia to Miss Hattie Weaver of Newark, NY.

Died: at Sodus Center, Nov. 12th, Mrs. Sally Morgan, ae 83 years.

Died: last Thursday, Mr. Yoemans of Manchester, son of the late honored merchant.

November 23, 1871
Married: in Clyde, Nov. 22nd, Flora Lamoreaux to James Vorhees.

Died: in Newark, Nov. 22nd, Mrs. Luke Agett, ae 73 years.

Died: Nov. 20th, Daniel Watrous, ae 76 yrs., one of Lyons oldest residents.

Died: Nov. 10th, Leman Gardner, ae 29 yrs., a citizen of Walworth - burial in Palmyra.

November 30, 1871
Married: in Lyons, Nov. 15th, Robert Walker of Arcadia to Anna Smith of Lyons.

Married: in Lyons, Nov. 22nd, William W. Cole and Luanna L. Bradley, dau. of John Bradley, Esq. of Lyons.

Married: on Nov. 18th, by Rev. Horace Eaton, Mr. Orrin Landon to Mrs. Evaline Heath, all of Palmyra.

Married: on Nov. 23rd, at Clyde, Mr. Aaron Griswold, and Miss Cornelia Wood.

Died: at Wacashma, MI, Nov. 22nd, W. W. Burgess, son-in-law of J. Leighton, Esquire, of Sodus. Burial in Vienna.

December 7, 1871
    Married: in Phelps, Nov. 29th, by Rev. J. C. Burgdorf, George E. Hornbeck to Rose Leroy, both of Phelps.

Married: on Nov. 23rd, J. Franklin Antisdale of Farmington to Miss Ella F. Brown of Macedon.

Died: at Alton, Nov. 28th, Samuel Snyder, ae 69 yrs.

Died: at Ontario, Wed. last, Lyman Cary, an old resident.

Died: at Ontario, Wed. last, Deacon William F. Gates.

December 21, 1871
    Married: in Marion, Dec. 7th, Francis C. Harness of Wiliamson, to Ella A., only dau. of Parley Hill, Esq.

Married: in Palmyra, Dec. 13th, Charles E. Powell to Carrie E. Lemunion, both of Manchester.

Died: in Walworth, Nov. 26th, Benjamin P. Wheeler, ae 19 yrs. 1 mo. 2 days.

Died: in Clyde, Dec. 5th, Sarah H., wife of Solomon H. Skinner, ae 57 yrs.

Died: in Lyons, Dec. 12, Mary, wife of John Gray, ae 57 years.

Died: in Lyons, Dec. 5th, Mary Gilkey, ae 71 years.

Died: in Huron, Dec. 5th, Benjamin S. Meeker, ae 62 years.

Died: at Palmyra, Dec. 19, Mr. Horace B. Lord, in his 63rd year.

Died: at Macedon, Dec. 10th, Joseph C. Parker, ae 45 years.

Died: in Newark, Mrs. James D. Ford.

Died: at Ontario: d. Dec. 2nd, Edward Miln, ae 73 years.

December 28, 1871
    Married: in Lyons, Dec. 14 (or 24?), Mr. Frederick Miller and Miss Lana Sutter, both of Lyons.

Married: in Palmyra, Dec. 7th, Mr. Charles I. Langworthy to Miss Emogene F. Bush, both of Marion.

Married: on Dec. 20th, by Rev. J. C. Burgdorf, Spencer Hooper to Miss Clara Burgess, both of Phelps.

Died: in Guthrie Center, Guthrie Co., IA, Dec. 7th, John Albert Sober, son of Jonathan and Mary Sober of Rose, NY, ae 23 years.

Died: in Ontario: William Smith d. Dec 22nd, ae 33 years.

January 4, 1872
Married: in Macedon, Dec. 27th, Leroy M. Baker of Walworth to Miss Elizabeth, dau. of Mr. Walter Lawrence of Macedon.

Married: in Palmyra, Dec. 27th, Mr. James Partridge to Miss Antoinette Rose, both of Manchester.

Married: in Palmyra, Dec 15th, Mr. Jay R. Finley of Walworth to Miss Ella J. Fillmore of Marion.

Married: in Palmyra, Dec 20th, Mr. William B. Wright to Miss Helen Hill, both of Walworth.

Married: at the Newark Methodist Church last Sabbath, Morgan L. Smith of Rose to Florine J. Crommett of Newark.

Married: in Manchester, Dec. 27th, by Rev. William Manning, Minard Robinson of Arcadia to Ella M. Rowe of Manchester.

Married: Dec. 27th by Rev. J. C. Burgdorf, G. H. Reaves of Mendon to Katie Richards of Newark.

Died: Mrs. S. D. Stone, d. in Butler, 2 weeks since.

January 11, 1872
Married: in Macedon, Jan. 1st, Mr. George A. Atwood of Webster, [Monroe Co.] to Miss Eva E. Palmer.

Married: in Arcadia, Dec. 25th, Mr. Andrew J. Beam of Sodus, to Harriet H. Depew of Arcadia.

Married: Jan 1st, Mr. Albert Seeley to Miss Ella C. Crane.

Married: Dec. 28th, William H. Edmondston of Farmington, to Alice A. Cole of Macedon.

Married: in Ontario, Dec. 27th, Mr. William Pane and Miss Electa Lane; also (same day?) m. Mr. Charles Baker and Miss Mary Hurley, both of Ontario.

Died: in Geneseo, Monday last, Gen. Craig Wadsworth, son of Gen. James S. Wadsworth, who fell in battle in the late war. Leaves a widow and one child.

Died: in Galen, NY, Dec. 27th, J. Coggeshall Peckham, age 36 years.

January 18, 1872
Married m. at East Newark, Dec. 28th, P. E. Nellis to Carrie Hooper.

Married: at East Newark, Jan. 10th, by Rev. A. H. Stearns, A. H. Chipman to Jennie E. Heath.

Married: on Jan. 3rd, George H. Everett of Palmyra and Carrie Smith of Walworth.

Died: in Palmyra, Wed., Mr. Durfee Chase, ae 79 yrs., oldest resident physician, member of the Episcopal Church 40 yrs.

Died: in Port Gibson, NY, Jan. 15th, Mary Ann, wife of George S. Snyder, ae 53 yrs.

Died: in Newark, Jan. 3rd, Mrs. John Harris, ae 63 years.

Died: at Palmyra, Jan. 7th, Mrs. Lucinda Knox, wife of Edward Knox, ae 51 years.

Died: in Rose, last Friday, Thomas Walton, brother of William Walton of Palmyra. Leaves a wife and family.

January 25, 1872
Married: m. in Macedon, Jan. 10th, Rueben T. Everett of Palmyra to Anna Augusta Beals, dau. of Ira Beals, Esq. of Macedon.

Married: in Lockport, Jan. 5th, Esbon [sic] B. Odell, of Newark to Miss Ida Zimmerman of Orangeport, NY.

Married: in Rose, Mr. M. A. Fisher, of Clyde to Miss Mary E. Garratt of Rose. [No date]

Married: in Lyons, Jan 17th, Mr. George T. Stanton and Miss Ruba E. McClellan.

Married: in East Newark, at the residence of P. Van Slyck, Jan 17th, by Rev. William Manning, Charles E. Tallmadge of Phelps and Carrie VanAlstine of East Newark.

Died: in Butler, on Thursday last, Mrs. Daniel Campbell.

February 1, 1872
Married in Newark, Jan. 24th, by Rev. S. Krum, Benjamin Shoales to Carrie Vibbard, all of Newark.

Died: in Galen, January 29th, Phebe A., wife of Mr. Job Travice, in her 68th year.

February 8, 1872
Married: on Feb. 6th, at the 3rd Presbyterian Church, Albany, NY, by Rev. E. Halley, D.D., T. Tobias Beckwith of New York, formerly of Newark, to Mary A. Hawley of Albany.

Married: in Walworth, Jan. 31st, John R. Newton of Marion, to Hattie, dau. of Rev. O. Eastman.

Married: at Newark, Jan. 24th, by Rev. A. C. Sewell, Salem G. Tinney to Avis G. Short, both of Newark.

Married: at Newark, Jan. 24th, by Rev. A. C. Sewell, William W. Beebe of Greenport, Long Island, to Mattie Short of Newark.

Married: at the residence of the bride's father, Jan. 31st, by Rev. W. H. Sloan, Erotus Warner to Ella M. Wake, dau. of John Wake, Esq., all of Marion.

Died: in Palmyra last Thursday, Mrs. Charles (Georgianna Cuyler) McLouth, last surviving child of Hon. George W. Cuyler, ae 31 yrs.

February 15, 1872
Died: in Newark, Feb. 11th, Mrs. Julia A. Pierce, ae 39 years.

Died: in Sodus, Feb. 12th, the widow of the late Benjamin Davis, ae 93 years.

February 22, 1872
Married: in Rochester, Jan. 31st, by Rev. R. D. Sproull, John G. Hislop of Palmyra to Nettie Pierce of Detroit [MI].

Married: in Lyons, Feb. 7th, by Rev. Mr. Jolley of Fairville, Thomas York and Cephese Barclay, dau. of Abram Barclay, Esq., both of Lyons.

Died: in Elmira, Jan. 31st, Hattie L., dau. of Rev. J. Alabaster.

Died: at Pultneyville, Feb. 13th, Hon. Samuel C. Cuyler, in his 63rd yr.

Died: Friday last, Miss Mary Simpson, dau. of Mr. James Simpson, ae 18 yrs.

Died: at New York, Roswell H. Jerome, ae 25 years.

Died: at Titusville, PA, Porter Lapham, son of the late John Lapham of Macedon.

Died: at Waterloo, Feb. 15th, Hon. Samuel Birdsall, ae 81 years.

February 29, 1872
Married: in DeWitt, IA, Feb. 14th, Frank Layton of Lyons, and Alice Gates of DeWitt [Onondaga Co.].

Died: in Ontario, Feb. 9th, J. S. Boynton, son of L. S. Boynton, ae 28 yrs.

Died: February 29, 1872: in Marion, Feb. 19th, Mr. Nathan L. Austen, ae 74 yrs.

Died: in Palmyra, Feb. 17th, Miss Tabitha Sheffield, ae 73 years.

March 7, 1872
Married: in Phelps, Feb. 20th, by Rev. William Manning, Frank Whitbeck of Palmyra and Ella Steadman of Phelps.

Married: in Arcadia Feb. 28th, by Rev. William Manning, Francis M. Filkins, of Phelps and Mary E. Whitney of Arcadia.

Married: in Phelps, on Feb. 22nd, Mr. E. Joseph Roys of Pultneyville, NY to Miss Amelia L. Combs of Geneva.

Married: in Newark, Feb. 28th, by Rev. J. C. Burgdorf, James McNeil of Phelps to Eliza Cook of Newark.

Died: in Arcadia Feb. 23rd, Mr. Charles Miller, ae 73 yrs., father of James H. Miller; his father, Samuel Miller was one of the earliest settlers in the town of Phelps.

Died: in Palmyra, Feb. 28th, Mrs. Sophia A. Richardson, ae 83 years.

Died: in Palmyra, Feb. 24th, Mehetable Eggleston, wife of Thomas Eggleston, ae 86 yrs 9 months.

Died: in California, Dec. 27th, Mr. James Jackson, second son of the late Stillman Jackson of Palmyra.

Died: at Palmyra, Feb. 26, Eli Benham, ae 55 years.

Died: in Rose, Feb. 22nd, Mrs. Sally, wife of Henry Garlick, ae 43 yrs.

Ontario deaths: a child of Peter Lyons ae 4 yrs; John Souden ae 22 yrs; John Boynton, ae 28 yrs.; Eli DeMarse, ae 36 yrs; John Denny, middle aged; Emma Reed, ae 15 yrs.; Mrs, Shepard, ae 53 yrs.

March 14, 1872
Married: in Lyons, Feb. 27th, by Rev. Dr. Samuel B. Bell, John Knobloch and Mary A. Hoyt, all of Lyons.

Married: in Newark, March 12th, by Rev. A. C. Sewall, Humphrey W. Covert to Emogene Alcorn, both of Phelps.

Died: in Lyons, Feb. 24th, Sally F., wife of Wilson Hoag in her 53rd yr.

Died: in Washington, Feb. 29th, Laura Louisa Whitney, ae 4 yrs. 7 mos., dau. of Leon and Lottie Whitney of Newark.

Died: in Sodus, March 6th, Mr. Robert Lund, ae 62 years.[The following deaths may also have taken place in Sodus]

Died: March 8th, Mr. B. B. Brayton, ae 59 yrs.; Mar. 3rd, infant child of Millard Boyd; on Mar 11th, at Sodus Point, Mrs S.S. Short, and infant; on Mar. 11th at Sodus Point, Andrew Wilbur, ae 60 yrs.

March 21, 1872
Married: by Rev. Charles Berry, David S. Cramer of Huron, to Mary A. McIntosh of Sodus.

Married: in Aylmer, Ontario, at Pine Lodge (residence of the bride's father), by Rev. William Ames, Mar. 7th, Chester F. Sturges of Lyons and Olive Wood, eldest dau. of Nathan L. Wood.

Died: in Rochester, Mar. 6th, Burton Searle, ae 24 yrs.

Died: at Sodus Point, Mar.11th, Nancy, wife of Seymour S. Short, ae 43 yrs 10 mos.

Died: in Fairmount, MN, Dec. 14th, 1871, Mrs. Catharine Ryder, wife of Willie Ryder, ae 41 yrs.

Died: in Buffalo, Mar. 7th, Harry, son of William H. and Amanda Baldwin, ae 1 mo. 7 days.

Died: in Lyons, March 7th, Mrs. Lydia Ellis, wife of B.V. Ellis, ae 56-10-6.

Died: in Pittsford, Hillsdale Co., MI, Feb. 29th, Mrs. Emogene Bump, dau. of John C. Roys, formerly of Lyons, ae 22 years.

Died: in South Butler, March 9th, Mrs. Anna Eliza Sweeting, wife of Volney H. Sweeting and dau. of Abram Dratt in her 21st yr.

Died: in Walworth, March 5th, Martha, wife of Samuel Strickland, ae 80 yrs.

Died: at the Hygienic Institution, Geneva, NY, March 11th, Caleb Smith, ae 89-7-8.

Died: in Geneva, March 13th, Mr. John Simpson, ae 83 years.

Ontario items: Died March 1, a dau. of George Miln, ae 9 yrs.; died on March 2nd, Charles Patterson, ae 74 yrs.; died on March 8th, Abraham Martin, ae 16 yrs.; d. March 10th, Anna Holmes, ae 15 yrs.; died March 12th, Doc. Carey, ae 96 yrs.; died March 15th, Mrs. Addison Turner.

Died: in Sodus, March 16th, Thomas Atkinson, ae 43 yrs.

March 28, 1872
Married: in Lockport, Mar. 14th, John H. Leach of Lyons and Maggie Warren of Lockport.

Married: at Clyde on Mar. 26th, George F. Millerd of Clyde to Miss Jennie Porter of Cazenovia, NY.

Died: March 25th, Jennie, dau. of David Ryckman, ae 10 years.

Died: in Chicago, Feb. 29th, Steven E. Whitlock, son of Nelson and Sarah Whitlock of Lyons, ae 26 yrs.

Died: in Lyons, March 18th, Charles S., son of Daniel W. and Henrietta J. Layton, in his 12th year.

Died: in Kalamazoo, MI, March 17th, Mrs. Jacob Mitchell, formerly of Lyons, ae 55 yrs.

Died: in Lyons, March 18th, Kate, wife of William H. Teller, ae 28 yrs.

Died: in Lyons, March 15th, Mrs. Felizidas Fuchs, ae 43 years.

April 4, 1872
Married: Mar. 20th by Rev. W. W. Runyon, Mr. Franklin L. Acker to Miss Lucy Ann Howard, all of Port Gibson.

Married: Mar. 31st, by Rev. W. W. Runyon, Mr. Jonathan Sibbet to Mrs. Martha A. Carlisle, all of Port Gibson.

Died: in New York, March 24th, Catharine, wife of William B. Miner, of New York City, and sister of Benjamin and Levi Whitlock of Lyons, ae 43 yrs.; burial in Lyons.

Died: in Lowell, MI, March 21st, Nathan D. Southard, formerly of Lyons, ae 56 yrs.

Died: in Butler, March 21st, Edward A., only son of Benham S. and S. Therissa Wood, ae 14-9-0.

Died: in Clyde, March 17th, Mary, wife of John Vosburgh and dau. of N. D. and M. E. Southard.

Died: in Palmyra, March 6th, Stephen Lake, ae 83 yrs.

April 11, 1872
Died: in the Town of Phelps, March 24th, Mrs. Mary Burnett, ae 83 yrs.

Died: at Anglo [Angola?], Erie Co., NY, March 25th, Mrs. William Shaw, ae 25 yrs, sister of Mrs. J. E. Cochran of Palmyra.

April 18, 1872
Married: Apr. 9th, Rev. C. L. Bown, Hale Gardner to Kate, dau. of John Boyd, Esq. of Sodus.

Married: at the M. E. Parsonage in East Palmyra, April 8th, by Rev.T. R. Green, Anton Niderer of Newark and Mary E. Rutherford of East Palmyra.

Died: in Palmyra, April 7th, Mr. James C. Fisk, ae 49 years.

Died: in Palmyra, April 10th, Mrs. Sarah Hollister, widow of the late Marvin Hollister, ae 33 years.

Died: in Phelps, April 5th, Ruth A. Leach, wife of Anson O. Leach, in her 66th year.

Died: in Pultneyville, March 30th, Randolph Reynolds, ae about 65 years.

Died: in Jonesville, MI, April 3rd, Alice, wife of Witter J. Baxter and dau. of the late Dr. A. L. Beaumont.

Died: in Lyons, April 9th, Charles H., only son of H. G. and Elizabeth G. Leach, ae 16-6-19.

Died: in Lyons, April 3rd, Mrs. Julia Ann Vanderbilt, aged 70 yrs. She was the dau. of William Paton of Lyons; her husband, Abram, died in his prime and left her with ten children. She was the mother of A. H. Vanderbilt of this place and of N. T. Vanderbilt of Lyons.

Died: on April 11th, near Fairville, Cleon E., son of Jacob E. and Rebecca J. Stever, ae 10 years.

April 25, 1872
Married: in Clifton Springs, April 10th, Henry Grace to Miss Maggie Lazenby.

Married: at Phelps, Apr. 17th, Walter A. Sibett to Miss Laura L. Reed.

The following deaths reported April 25th took place in Phelps: Mrs. Ruth Ann Leach; Williams Spencer, ae 15 yrs; Mrs. Mary Barton; Mrs. Mary A. White; Charles C., son of John T. Watkins; Mrs. Thankful Joslyn.

Died: at Clifton, Mrs. Cyrus D. Prince.

Died: at Plainville, [Onondaga Co.], David Peer, ae 84 years.

Died: in Lyons, April 16th, Eliza Agnes, dau. of George Ernst in her 17th yr.

Died: in Lyons, April 11th, Henry Grimm, native of Alsace, Germany, aged 90 yrs.

Died: in Palmyra, April 2nd, Victor, son of Philip I. Feller, ae 15 yrs.

Died: in Lyons, April 12th, Charles, son of Henry Smith, ae 10 yrs.

Died: Palmyra, April 18th, David Sanford.

Died: in Palmyra, April 11th, Nelson G., son of H. H. North, ae 17 years.

Died: in Palmyra, April 16th, James Seeley, ae 68 yrs.

Died: in Palmyra, April 12th, Allen Williams, ae 66 yrs.

Died: at Shortsville, April 21, Mrs. Huldy Kipp, wife of J. H. Kipp and dau. of L. Runyon of Newark, ae 34 years.

Died: in Newark, April 20th, Mrs. Susan Robinson, ae 48 years.

Died: in Arcadia, April 19th, Richard, eldest son of P. K. Shaw.

Died: at Sodus, April 20th, widow of the late _____ DeRight, ae 55 yrs.

Died: at Joy, April 20th, Emma, dau. of C. Wells.

Died: April 20th at Pultneyville, April 20th, George, son of Elias Cady, ae 24 yrs.

Died: April 22nd, Rev. William H. Ward, Sr., ae 82 years.

Died: April 20th, Michael Bean, ae 18 years.

May 2, 1872
Married: in Port Gibson, April 7th, by Rev. W. W. Runyon, Mr. Charles Babcock to Miss Mary E. Shannon.

Married: at the residence of the bride's parents, April 24th, by Rev. W. W. Runyon, Mr. Adelbert H. King to Miss Anna Post, all of Manchester, Ontario Co., NY.

Married: in Lyons, April 22nd, Mr. George F. Marsh of Holley, NY, and Miss Kate Mansfield of Lyons.

Married: in Red Creek, Mar. 30th, at the dwelling of Amos Snyder, Robert Reynolds of Sodus, and Miss Lorena Crego of Butler.

Married: m. April 28th, at the house of John Dutcher, Esq., of Wolcott, Edgar Gardner of Syracuse and Miss Ann Moore of Wolcott.

Married: in Clyde, April 24th, Mr. George R. McClellan of Seneca Falls and Miss Alma Hendee Youngs, of Clyde.

Married: in Palmyra May 1st, Mr. Henry W. Southwick and Miss Julia E. Anderson.

Married: in Palmyra Mr. William G. Hislop and Miss Mary L. Tanner. [no date]

Died: d. in Lyons, April 22nd, William, son of Samuel Bellinger, ae 4 yrs.

Died: in Lyons, April 24th, Eva, wife of B. Bonacker, ae 52 years.

Died: in Lyons, April 19, Charles, eldest son of Charles Winter, ae 9 years.

Died: in Milwaukee, WI, April 20th, Dr. George W. Perrine, in his 56th yr.

May 9, 1872
Died: in Phelps, May 2nd, Carrie S., wife of H. N. Roberts and dau. of P. McGregor of Newark.

Died: in Lyons, April 20th, Louis, son of Henry and Julia Grimm, ae 1 year.

Died: in Lyons, April 30th, George H., eldest son of Henry and Hannah Wolrath [sic], ae 33 years.

Died: in Lyons, April 27th, John Homewood, ae 59 yrs.

Died: in Butler, April 26th, Ida, dau. of Charles McGonigal, ae 59 years.

Died: in Lyons, April 22nd, Margaret Ann, dau. of Alvah and Ann Brundage, ae 37 years.

Died: in Clyde, April 24th, Ella, youngest dau. of J. E. Tramper, in her 21st year.

Died: in Galen, April 26th, Phebe, wife of Mott Stafford (deceased), ae 43 yrs.

Died: in Marion, April 26, Solomon West, ae 72 years.

May 9, 1872
   Died: in Palmyra, April 28th, Melissa, wife of Gurdon T. Smith, ae 65 years.

Died: in East Newark, May 3rd, Eunice E. Hill, adopted dau. of Peter Hill, ae 14 yrs. 6 mos.

Died: in E. Newark, May 5th, William H., son of Anthony and Caroline Hill, ae 7 yrs 2 mos.

Died: in East Newark, May 6th, Eliza Houser, ae 53 yrs.

May 16, 1872
   Married: May 1st, Mr. Orrin Barrow and Mrs. Elizabeth Dietz, both of Palmyra.

Died: d. in Lyons, May 6th, Able M. Mastin, son of Stephen H. Mastin, ae 4 years

Died: in Clyde, May 3rd, Mrs. M. Bircher, ae 67 years.

Died: in Sodus, May 4th, Hiram Thompson.

Died: in Galen, May 2nd, Silas Reynolds, ae 46 yrs.

May 23, 1872
   Died: in Palmyra, May 10th, Mrs. Harriet H. Rogers, relict of Gen. Thomas Rogers, in her 85th year.

Died: d. in Arcadia, May 16th, Harry Weaver, ae 67 years.

Died: d. May 16th at Allegan, MI, William C. Messenger, son of Edward Messenger of Sodus, ae 44 years.

May 30, 1872
   Married: in Palmyra, May 22nd, Mr. Fahy of Rochester, and Miss Kitty Welch of Palmyra.

Married: in Prattsburg, NY, May 23rd, Mr. John N. Brownell of Lyons and Miss Sara P. Ardell, of the former place.

Married: in Lyons, May 16th, Mr. Charles H. Roys and Miss Julia K. Holley of Lyons.

Died: in Newark, Frank E., only son of Mr. and Mrs. G. L. Lewis, at the age of 18 years.

Died: in Clyde, May 10th, E. O. Grady, ae 23 years.

Died: in Marengo, May 10th, Myron Pellys, ae 47 years.

Died: In Galen, May 13th, Demas Blakeman, ae abt. 75 years.

Died: in Sodus, May 19th, George W. Sanford, ae 43 years.

Died: in Lyons, May 20th, Henry, youngest son of George and Abby Ernst ae 2 yrs. and also on Apr. 16th, Eliza Agnes, dau. of the same, ae 16 years.

Died: at Palmyra, May 18th, Sanford P. Calhoun, ae 69 years.

Died: at Port Gibson, May 10th, Nellie, infant dau. of W. W. Hough, ae 14 months.

Died: in Phelps, May 12th, Joseph M. Goseline, ae 30 years.

Died: in Sodus Center, May 19th, William Frederick, eldest son of Fred K. Metz, ae 8 years.

Died: d. in Clyde, May 19th, Mrs. Sallie Watson, ae 97 years.

June 6, 1872
Died: in Joy, May 21st, John M. Dennison, ae 22 years.

Died: in Hillsdale, MI, May 26th, George E. Allen, formerly of Port Gibson.

Died: in New Orleans, May 1st, W. H. Lester, formerly of Clyde, age 28 years.

Died: in Clyde, May 29th, William, son of M. G. and Sophia Ely, ae 6 years.

Died: in Clyde, May 28th, Mrs. A. Pardee, ae 38 years.

Died: in Clyde, May 27th, Mrs. B. Lux, ae 37 years.

June 13, 1872
Married: in Rochester, May 20th, Charles H. Aldrich of Farmington to Miss Charlotte Cobb of Phelps, NY.

Married: at Newark, June 5th, by Rev. A. C. Sewall, Calvin W. Bryant to Kate E. Stevens, both of Newark.

Died: last Saturday, Mrs. Willis Brownell.

Died: at Palmyra, June 4th, Joseph C. Lovett, ae 59 years.

Died: in Cazenovia, [Madison Co., NY], May 27th, Clara May, dau. of Irving C. and Emily E. Forte, ae 10 years.

Died: in Phelps, May 20th, George W. W. Blinn, ae 44 years.

Died: in Lyons, June 1st, Mrs. Bridget Hopkins, ae 51 years.

Died: in Williamson, June 1st, Charles Smith, ae 30 years.

Died: in Phelps, May 27th, Miss Sarah Ann Deming, ae 65 years.

Died: in Phelps, June 6th, William R. Ray, ae 66 years, brother of the Hon. Henry Ray.

Died: at Geneva, May 29th, Sarah A., wife of R. S. Drake, ae 29 years.

Died: at Sodus, June 6th, Mr. Peter Brant, ae 78 yrs., citizen [of Sodus] for 40 yrs.

June 20, 1872
Married: in Lockport, by Rev. J. M. Harris, June 5th, John M. Ives of Rochester to Sarah E. White of Lockport.

Married: in Palmyra by Rev. H. A. Eaton, June 11th, William Dickie of Lyons and Emily White of Palmyra.

Died: in Butler, May 29th, Mrs. M. P. Blakesley, ae about 50 years.

Died: in Galen, June 8th, Lewis Waterbury, in his 75th year.

Died: in "Center" [?], May 22nd, Mrs. John Proseus, in her 79th year.

Died: in Butler, June 6th, William Wood, ae 80 years.

Died: at Alcott, June 9th, Sarah Bullard, wife of Hamilton Bullard, formerly of Lyons, ae 52 years. [This editor was unable to find a village/city with the name, Alcott, in NY or the U.S. The name may have been an error in the original publication and should actually be Wolcott, NY.]

Died: in Sodus Point, June 6th, Miss Rose Willig of Philadelphia, sister of the late Mrs. Georgiana Lummis. Burial in St. Peter's Church in Phildelphia.

June 27, 1872
Married: in Rose, June 12th, Marcus Baker and Mary D. Genung, both of Rose.

Died: in Marion, June 17th, Mr. Noah Cressy, ae 63 years.

Died: in Lyons, June 15th, Alice M., dau. of Isaac Barton, ae 16 years.

Died: in Butler, June 12th, Jude Lampman, ae 56 years.

July 3, 1872
Married: in Ontario on June 27th, by Rev. N. Bosworth at the residence of the bride's parents, M. J. Elam Tufts to Miss Mary G. Albright.

Married: at Phelps, June 26th, Mr. George St. Clair, of Michigan to Miss Rose A. Howe of Phelps.

Died: in Williamson, June 20th, Mrs. Frank E. Williams of Buffalo, dau. of S. S. Peppino, Esq., ae about 33 years.

Died: in Sodus, June 23rd, Simeon Knapp, ae about 40 years.

Died: in Lyons, June 20th, Luther C. Hosford, ae 71 years.

July 11, 1872
Married: June 27th, at the residence of George W. Cuyler, Esq., by Rev. John G. Webster, Thomas Posse and Susan Anscomb, both of Palmyra.

Died: at Palmyra, June 29th, Nancy Van Ostrand, ae 66 years.

Died: at Marion, July 1st, James H. Curtis, ae 72 years.

Died: two children of Mr. John M. Drake, Of Palmyra, struck by lightning; one age 3 years..

July 18, 1872
Died: in Palmyra, July 8th, Miss Nancy Johnson, ae 79 years.

Died: in Marion, July 5th, Lydia, wife of Joseph Dickenson, ae 35 years.

Died: in the Town of Manchester, July 2nd, Minerva M. Miner, ae 26 years.

July 25, 1872
Married: in Macedon, July 14th, Mr. Addison Fuller of Macedon to Miss P. M. Aldrich of Hudson, MI.

Married: June 25th, T. S. Ostrander of Castleton, NY and Carrie J. Cronise of Arcadia.

Married: at the residence of the bride, July 16th, by Rev. W. W. Runyan, Mr. George S. Snyder to Mrs. Ann H. Miller, all of Port Gibson.

Died: in Wolcott, July 7th, Milton Dempsey, in the 27th yr. of his age.

Died: in Clyde, July 13, Harriet M., wife of Peter Simons in her 32nd year.

Died: in Newark, July 15th, Levi Pulver, ae 73 years.

August 1, 1872
Married: at Palmyra on July 18th, Miss Fannie E. Bortles to Charles Drowne.

Married: July 16th, Max G. Green of Chicago, IL to Miss Louise E. Aldrich, formerly of Palmyra.

Died: in Clyde, July 20th, Jesse, son of Lemuel Lape, ae 4 years

Died: in Clyde, July 21st, Mrs. James Burgess, ae about 55 years.

Died: in Newark, July 20, Catharine M., wife of William Fleming, ae 55 years.

Died: near Hydesville, July 28, John J. Smith, ae 77 years. [Hyndesville, Schoharie Co.?]

Died: at Ontario, July 29th, Addison Turner.

August 8, 1872
　　Married: in Walworth, Aug. 4th, Mr. Edgar Perrin to Miss Sarah A. Cone.

Died: in Palmyra, July 25, Albert Butts, ae 29 years.

Died: in Cleveland, OH, Mrs. Abiah H. Reeves, widow of Zebulon Reeves, formerly of Palmyra, ae 77 years.

Died: in Newark, Aug. 3rd, Howell Bidwell Gunnison, son of William W. and Sarah B. Gunnison, and gr. son of the late Gen. D. D. Bidwell, of Buffalo, ae 4 years.

Died: at Sodus Center, July 27th, Caroline Watson, ae 61 years.

Died: at Palmyra, Aug. 6th, Mabel, a child of Eugene and Ellen Smith, ae 2 years.

Died: At Elizabethtown, KY, Aug. 5th, Albert W., son of Mathew Wigglesworth of Macedon, ae 24 years.

Died: in Lyons, Aug. 5 Mr. Samuel Cole, ae 67 years.

August 22, 1872
　　Married: on Aug. 14th, at the residence of the bride's father, by Rev. Albert H. Potter, Mr. E. B. Rew of Buffalo, formerly of Newark to Miss Mollie E. Gordon of Silver Creek.

Died: Aug. 15th, James Bagley, father of W. B. Williams of Newark, ae 92 years.

Died: in Lyons, Aug. 12th, Robert, youngest son of John H. Bourne, ae 1 yr. 3 months.

Died: in Clyde, Aug. 13th, Smith German, ae about 30 years.

Died: in Sodus, Aug. 8th, Charles Knox, ae 79 years.

Died: in Lyons, Aug. 13th, Abel Lyman, ae 76 years.

Died: in Wolcott, Aug.10th, Lena, wife of George Shaver, ae 58 years.

August 29, 1872
　　Died: in Marion, Aug. 22, Rebecca, widow of the late Gardner Hicks, ae 77 years.

Died: in Palmyra, Aug. 18th, Helen P. Williams, wife of Clark S. Chase, only dau. of Richard S. Williams, ae 38 years.

September 5, 1872
Married: in Palmyra on Aug. 29th, Mr. N. G. Drake and Miss Matie E. Johnson, dau. of David Johnson, Jr.

Married: at the residence of Mr. W. R. Folwell in Newark, by Rev. J. S. Blanden, Aug. 27th, Mr. Henry Lienhart to Miss Laura A. French, both of Newark.

Died: in Marion, Aug. 14th, Viola Grimes, dau. of Myron E. Grimes, ae 13 years.

Died: in Butler, Aug. 18th, Vila B., dau. of D. N. Miner, ae 15-9-0.

Died: at Lyons, Aug. 22nd, Allie Bell, youngest dau. of James W. Vandeberg, ae 10 months.

Died: in Phelps, Aug. 28th, Spencer Mead, son of John Stonebridge, ae 11 years.

Died: in Newark, Sept. 2nd, Georgia May, twin dau. of Smith W. and Mary Sanford, ae 10 months.

Died: Aug. 21st, Calvin, son of Titus Newport, ae 21 years.

September 12, 1872
Married: in Palmyra, Sept. 4th, Mr. Louis M. Chase and Miss Anna L. Page, only dau. of W. F. Page.

Married: in Palmyra, Sept. 4th, Mr. A. J. Hopkins of Oswego, NY to Mrs. A. E. Wells of Palmyra.

Married: in Canandaigua, Aug. 11th, Mr. William A. Power and Miss Hannah Pritchard.

Married: in Unadilla Forks, NY, Aug. 25th, Mr. H. Dwight Bassett and Miss Flora E. Wilcox.

Married: by Rev. William Manning, Sept. 4th, at the residence of the bride's parents, in Newark, Mr. George H. Bentley of Glens Falls, NY and Miss Frankie S. Burgett of Newark.

Married: at Newark on Sept. 10th, by Rev. J. C. Burgdorf, Mr. Jay S. Vary of Churchville and Miss Addie M. Abbott of Newark.

September 12, 1872

Died: in Marion, Aug. 31st, Mrs. Catharine R. Tiffany, widow of the late Edwin Tiffany, ae 68 years

Died: in Girrard, MI, Aug. 25th, Jane E. Arnold, dau. of Casper and Lucy Hollenbeck, formerly of Palmyra.

Died: at Palmyra, Aug. 21st, George Williams, son of Charles Walton, ae 1 year.

Died: at Shortsville, Sept. 3rd, Mr. Charles Hudson, ae 72 years.

Died: at Galen, Aug. 30th, Maria, wife of Col. P.V.N. Smith, ae 76 years.

Died: in Savannah, Aug. 31st, Mrs. Exner, ae 44 years.

Died: in Clyde, Sept. 4th, Orlando Haight, ae about 40 years.

Died: in Clyde, Aug. 31st, Mrs. Mulligan, ae about 50 years.

Died: in Sodus, Elizabeth Malcomb, Sept. 8th, ae about 22 years.

Died: in Niagara, Cornelius Brewster, Sept. 8th, ae about 55 yrs., formerly of Williamson.

September 26, 1872

Married: in Savannah, Sept. 18th, Mr. Robert E. Goodwin and Miss Emma G. [C?] Pomeroy.

Died: in Jasper Co., MO, Aug. 20th, Ruth, wife of Luther Sanford, and sister of Mr. Stephen Culver of Newark.

Died: in Galen, Sept. 17th, Erastus Miles, ae 82 years

Died: in Clyde, Sept. 14th, an infant child of John Shindler.

Died: in Clyde, Sept. 14th, William, son of Thomas Arzberger, ae 19 months.

Died: in Galen, Sept. 14th, Stephen, son of Jeffery Collins, ae 8 months.

Died: in Rose, Sept. 18th, Hosea Daniels, ae 91 years.

Died: in East Newark, Sept. 24th, Miss Nellie Rose, dau. of the Honorable L. L. Rose.

October 3, 1872
Married: in Arcadia, Sept. 25th, Mr. W. M. White of Williamson and Alice Westfall of Arcadia.

Died in Syracuse, Sept. 7th, Joseph Clarke, ae 59-9-0.

Died: in Galen, Sept. 24th, James Rhumbolt, ae 53 years.

Died: in Clyde, Sept. 24th, Fanny Rodwell, ae 18 years.

Died: in Rose, Sept. 23rd, Charles D. Wykoff, ae 10 yrs.

Died: in Clyde, Sept. 23rd, Anna Kirby, ae 3 years.

Died: in Lyons, Sept. 21st, Eliza Raddar, ae 7 years.

Died: in Phelps, Sept. 26th, Mr. Henry Bell, ae 78 years.

Died: in Junius, Sept. 21st, Deborah Cuddeback, ae 64 years.

Died: at the residence of her daughter, Mrs. A. J. Price, at Clarkson, Monroe Co., NY, Sept. 10th, Mrs. Jane Jackson, wife of the late Dr. Cyrus Jackson of Lyons, NY, ae 83 years.

Died: at his residence on Canandaigua Road, Sunday last, William A. Partridge, Esq., ae (?).

Died: at the Rectory of Christ Church, Rochester, Mrs. Anna Davidson Battershall, wife of Rev. Walton W. Battershall, and dau. of Fletcher Williams of Newark, ae 29 yrs. 6 months.

Died: at Newark, Sept. 18th, George Ray Sanford, only son of S. W. and Mary Sanford, ae 10 mos. 5 days.

October 10, 1872
Married: in Lyons, Oct. 2nd, by Rev. T. B. Hudson, Mr. George Z. Taylor to Miss Rose Agett, all of Lyons.

Married: m. at Clifton Springs, Sept. 30th, Wakeman T. Nickerson of Bernhards Bay, NY, to Mary L. Cox of Clifton Spa.

Married: in Williamson, Oct. 2nd, by Rev. John Wilder, Mr. Thomas Nichols to Miss Deborah Maines.

Died: in Clyde, Sept. 30th, William H. Robinson, ae about 35 years.

Died: in Palmyra, Sept. 20th, Humphrey Sherman, ae 58 years.

Died: in Lyons, Sept. 25th, Charles Henry, oldest son of Henry and Magdalena Barral, ae 12-11-20.

Died: in Kendallville, IN, Sept. 21st, Mrs. F. M. Akenhead, wife of Thomas Akenhead, deceased, ae 72 years.

Died: in Linn Co., MO, Sept. 4th, William H. Griswold, late of Rose, and brother of L. Griswold, of Lyons, ae 52 years.

Died: in East Newark, Oct. 8th, Mrs. Ezra Chadwick, ae 66 years.

October 17, 1872
Married: m. at the residence of the bride's father, Ransom Allerton, by Rev. William Manning, Oct. 16th, Mr. Seneca Short to Miss Florence Allerton.

Married: at Palmyra, Oct. 10th, Mr. William L. Moore to Miss Gertie Beach, all of Palmyra.

Died: in Butler, Oct.3rd, George Fowler, son of William Fowler, ae 28 years.

Died: at Palmyra, Oct. 8th, Leroy Hulburt, ae 24 yrs.

Died: at Palmyra, Oct. 4th, A. H. Wentworth, Esq., ae 68 years.

Died: at Williamson, Oct. 5th, Samuel Hance, ae 92 yrs., one of the earliest settlers, locating in Farmington in 1803, father of Benjamin Hance of Williamson, one of the Board of Supervisors of Wayne Co.

Died: at Ontario, Oct. 8th, Sarah Saunders, dau. of Joseph Saunders, ae 24 years..

October 24, 1872
Married: at Palmyra, Oct. 22nd, John F. Colburn of Geneva, to Miss Fannie L. Clemons of Palmyra.

Married: at Sodus, Sept. 26, by E. W. Kelly, Esq., Daniel Plumb of Huron and Mrs. Laura A. Diddy.

Died: in the town of Arcadia, Oct. 17th, Mary Lux, ae 23-2 6.

Died: at Adrian, MI, Oct. 11th, Julia, wife of T. G. Mead, and dau. of John N. Brownell, Esq., of Macedon, ae 20 years.

Died: near Prince Edward Co., VA, Sept. 28th, Louisa T., wife of Calvin H. Bliss, formerly of Clyde, ae 63 years.

Died: at Titusville, PA, Oct. 10th, Elmira E., eldest dau. of James Rice, ae 35 yrs.

Died: at Palmyra, Oct. 12th, in his 66th year, Rev. Sylvester Adams.

Died: at Marcy, Oct. 10, Miss Caroline M. Williams, ae 58 years.

Died: on Oct. 18th, Jane E., wife of John J. Shufelt, ae 75 yrs. 10 months.

Died: in the village of Clyde, Oct. 11th, in the 39th year of her age, Lucy Louisa, wife of Samuel S. Morely.

October 31, 1872
Died: in Galen, Oct. 22nd, Miss Susan Powers, ae 79 years.

Died: in Lyons, Oct. 12th, William H. Rinkel, son of Michael and Eva Rinkel, ae 15 years.

Died: in Lyons, Oct. 14th, Josi A., youngest son of Gottfried and Magdalena Czerny, ae 3 yrs. 12 days.

Died: in Marion, Oct. 9th, Cynthia Congdon, ae 20 years.

Died: in Lyons, Oct. 19th, Julia A. Hoetzel, age 33 yrs., a resident of California.

Died: d. in Valpariso, IN, Oct. 10th, Mrs. Hannah Sergeant, mother of Mrs. James A. Boyd of Sodus, ae 65 years.

Died: October 19th, William Sherman, ae 52 years.

Died: at West Lynn, MA, Sept. 19th, Stephen P. W. Douglass, ae 68 yrs. Burial in Williamson.

Died: Friday last, Mrs. Benjamin Hill, ae 68 years.

November 14, 1872
    Married: m. at Macedon Center, Nov. 2nd, by E. Bogardus, Esq., Charles Lincoln to Miss Ella Martin, both of Macedon.

Died: in Yorkville, OH, Nov. 4th, Clintie M., son of Samuel and Nellie Bloomer, ae 8 yrs 6 mos. (S. M. & H. A. S. Bloomer) [sic]

November 21, 1872
    Married: in Lima, NY, Oct. 31st, James T. Gilmore of Phelps to Nellie J. Claven of Lima.

Married: in Phelps, Nov. 6th, John Haight of Corning and Mary Lynch of Phelps.

Married: in Phelps, Nov. 6, Mr. Jonathan Moule of Riga, to Miss Hattie Robinson of Phelps.

Married: in Phelps, Nov. 13th, Mr. Edward Sherman to Miss Ella, dau. of John Yeo.

Died: in Galen, Nov. 5th, Thomas Flynn, ae 22 years.

Died: in Clyde, Nov. 5th, Mrs. Nancy Fairchild, ae 84 years.

Died: in Palmyra, Oct. 26th, Simon H. Veeder, ae 68 yrs.

Died: in Palmyra, Oct. 29th, John Murray, ae 45 years.

Died: Nov. 5th, Libbie, wife of Charles Bigelow, ae 38 years.

November 28, 1872
    Married: m. in Palmyra, Nov. 20th, George S. Beadle of Palmyra, to Adelia Philips.

Married: in Palmyra, Nov. 15th, Lewis E. Taber of Binghamton and Miss Sarah M. Smith.

Died: in Wolcott, Nov. 13th, Mrs. N. Cromwell.

Died: in Lyons, Nov. 6th, Richard Van Benschoten, in his 66th year.

Died: in Arcadia, Nov. 18th, James Pollock, one of the earliest settlers in Lyons, in his 83rd year.

Died: in Sodus, Nov. 18th, Emanuel Stone, ae 70 years.

Died: in Belle Plain, IA, Nov. 17th, wife of Sidney S. Sweet of that place, and dau. of Mr. A. Lyman of Lyons.

December 5, 1872
Married: m. in Palmyra, Nov. 21st, L. Hinton, M.D. of Washington, AR to M. Augusta Montrose.

Married: on Nov. 21st, Miss Ellen Shockly to Mr. George Wixon of Ohio.

Married: in Palmyra, Nov. 26th, Mr. J. Angell of Odell, IL, to Miss Mary Parker of Palmyra.

Married: in South Sodus, Nov. 6th, Mr. Giles Fonda, of South Sodus to Miss Ida Messenger, of LyonS.

Married: by Rev. A. H. Shurtleff, Andrew Walhizer and Miss Elizabeth Espencheid, all of Sodus.

Married: at Ontario, Nov. 20th, Dr. P. Redner of Colorado, to Miss M. O. Hill, of Ontario.

Married: on Nov. 26th, by Rev. A. C. Sewall, Mr. Samuel A. Pierson to Miss Lizzie O. Crosby, both of Newark.

Died: in Marion, Nov. 24th, Mrs. Elizabeth Skinner, consort of Mr. Warren Skinner.

Died: in Lyons, Mary Berns, niece of Henry Berns, and recently from Germany, ae 17 yrs.

Died: in Lyons, Nov. 22nd, Eva Rinkel, dau. of Michael and Eva Rinkel, in her 18th year.

Died: in Galen, Nov. 26th, Joseph C. Watson, ae 76 years.

Died: in Palmyra, Nov. 15th, Henry Vandyne, ae 57 years.

Died: in Arcadia, Nov. 30th, Miss Nancy Corwin, ae 77 years.

December 12, 1872
Married: in Clyde at the Presbyterian Church by Rev. J. R. Young, on Dec. 4th, Mr. William McMath of Holmesville, LA, and Miss Mary Smith, dau. of Thomas Smith, Esq. of Clyde.

Married: in Lyons, Dec. 4th, Mr. Orselah W. Baxter and Miss Mary R. Otto, both of Lyons.

Married: in Lyons, Dec. 4th, Mr. Aaron C. Stevens, of Lock Berlin and Miss Lucy M. Rogers of Lyons.

Married: in Rochester, Nov. 27th, by Rev. Dr. Short, Mr. Charles G. Elliott to Miss Ella Watters, both of Clyde.

Married: in Port Gibson, Dec. 5th, By Rev. W. W. Runyan, Mr. J. A. Steverson of Junius to Miss Diantha D. Willson of Port Gibson.

Died: in Pultneyville, Nov. 23rd, John Dunning, ae abt. 25 years.

Died: in Junius, at the residence of his father-in-law, Nov. 27th, Abram S. Braden, of Marengo, ae 25 years.

Died: at Marion, Nov. 29th, Anderson G., infant son of Rev. W. H. and Ada A. Sloan, ae 3 mos. 23 days.

December 19, 1872
Married: Nov. 26th, in Phelps, Mr. Frank O. Kent of Geneva to Miss Florence L. Cummings of Phelps.

Married: in Palmyra, Dec. 8th, Mr. Charles A. Beswick, to Miss Kittie L. Fuller, both of Rochester.

Married: in Macedon, Dec. 10th, Oren B. Covell of Ticonderoga, NY, to Miss Harriet Wolvin of Macedon.

Married: in Manchester, Dec. 5th, J. Lyre, Jr. to Miss Libbie M. Tilden.

Married: in Rochester, Dec. 14th, Mr. Eli Jepson to Miss Ellen Ward, both of Savannah, NY.

Died: in Lyons, Dec. 6th, James Agett, ae 83 years.

Died: in Rochester, Dec. 6th, Charles Koester, ae 35 years.

December 26, 1872
Married: Dec. 11th, in New Gloucester, ME, Rev. Anson S. Titus, Jr. of Phelps, to Miss Lucy T. Merrill.

Married: at Marion, Dec. 17th, Mr. White to Miss Mary Tassell.

Married: in Phelps on Dec. 18th, Mr. Edward T. Ray, of Coldwater, MI, to Miss Carrie A. Titus, of Phelps.

Married: at Palmyra, Dec. 18th, Murganzy Hopkins to Rebecca S. Butterfield.

Died: at Palmyra, Andrew Cragin, a native of Ireland, ae 78 years.

Died: Dec. 14th, Arthur D. Walbridge, eldest son of S.D. and Maria Walbridge, ae 29-8-0.

Died: Dec. 22nd, Emma P., dau. of J. P. and Anna L. Vandusen, of Newark, ae 6 yrs. 2 months.

January 1, 1873
Married: at the residence of the bride's mother, Dec. 25th, by Rev. W. W. Runyon, Mr. Stephen Snyder to Miss Martha H. Moore , all of Port Gibson, NY.

Married: at the residence of the bride's parents, Dec 25th, Mr. Charles Huntoon, to Miss Amelia Terry, all of Port Gibson, NY.

Married: at Sodus, Dec. 18th, Mr. Allen Jones and Miss Lottie E. Fillenham.

Married: at Ontario, Dec. 25th, Mr. N. J. Fenster to Miss Julia Brown, all of Ontario.

Married: in Lyons, Dec. 31st, Mr. J. Myron Curtiss of Winfield, NY to Miss Mary Bottom of Lyons.

Married: in Erie, PA, Dec. 24th, Mr. M. D. L. Buell of Kirkwood, MO and Miss Libbie Denier of Lyons.

Married: in South Butler, Dec. 24th, Mr. James A. Ackerman to Miss Helen E. Doty of South Butler.

Died: in Palmyra, Dec. 25th, Betsey Harkness, ae 79 yrs.

Died: in Galen, Dec. 23rd, Henry C. Van Amburgh, ae 67 years.

Died: at Stebbensville, Ionia Co., MI, Dec. 22nd, Josephus Stebbins, son of C.A. Stebbins, of Newark, ae 49-2-5 days.

Died: in Fairville, Dec. 15th, William C., son of Abraham A. and Mary Dubois, ae 2 yrs. 9 months.

January 15, 1873
Died: Jan. 9th, Mrs. James P. Bartle, resident of Newark about 50 yrs.

Died: in Rose, Dec. 25th, Peter Rihn, ae 21 years.

Died: in Athens, NY, Nov. 29th, Miss Lydia Goldsmith formerly of Lyons, in her 83rd year.

Died: in Lyons, Dec. 30th, Emma, dau. of Michael and Eva Rinkel, ae 13-3-3 days.

Died: at the residence of her son-in-law, M. M. Kenyon, in Newark, Mrs. Louisa B., widow of the late James P. Bartle, ae 69-6-10.

January 23, 1873
Married: in Palmyra, Jan. 6th, Mr. Charles Ross to Miss Selinda Watkins, both of Manchester.

Married: in Palmyra, Jan. 8th, Mr. Charles W. Latimer of Norwich, Chenango Co., to Miss Ella A. Bacus.

Married: in Marion, Jan. 15th, Mr. Owen Mann of Ann Arbor, MI, to Miss Belle Ford.

Married: in Clifton, Jan. 19th, Mr. Jerome C. Haynes of Lyons and Miss Ella Wood of Clifton [Monroe Co].

Married: in Phelps, Jan. 22nd, by Rev. William Manning, Alonzo Newton of Junius, and Carrie Hickson of Phelps.

Married: at Rural Grove, Montgomery Co., NY on Jan. 23rd, by Rev. J. O. Burgdorf, father of the bride, William S. L. Frear to Miss Martia I. Burgdorf.

Died: in Palmyra, Jan. 14th, Darius Pullman, in his 82nd yr. and on the same day, his wife, Louisa, ae 80 years.

Died: at Jackson, Mi, Jan. 15th, Charles H. VanDyne, ae 33 years.

January 23, 1873: d. on Jan. 16th, Mrs. Henry Novess (?), ae 73 years.

January 30, 1873
Died: in Williamson, Jan. 12th, John O'Byne, ae about 45 years.

Died: in Waterloo, Jan. 25th, Mrs. Graves, widow of the late John B. Graves, and recently of Williamson ae 50 years.

Died: in Pultneyville, Jan. 12th, Richard Craggs, ae about 85 years.

Died: in Waterloo, Jan. 14th, Patrick Moran, ae 73 years.

Died: in Odell, IL , Jan. 15th, Nathan Angell, formerly a resident of Galen, in his 71st yr.

****

The item below was evidently added to this work as an aside from these newspaper abstracts.

"An old tombstone in the cemetery next to the schoolhouse No. 7 District: "Sacred to [the Memory of] William Hopkins and Eunice, his wife, who d. July 17, 1893...William aged 67 and Eunice, 58."

INDEX

Abbott, Addie M., 45
Abbott, Rev., 7
Acker, Franklin L., 35
Ackerman, James A., 53
Adams, Carrie C., 20
Adams, Carrie M., 20
Adams, Charles R., 20
Adams, Sylvester, 49
Agans, Elias, R., 14
Agett, Luke, 27
Agett, Rose, 47
Agett, James, 52
Akenhead, F. M., 48
Akenhead, Thomas, 48
Alabaster, Hattie L., 31
Alabaster, J., 31
Albright, Mary G., 42
Alcorn, Emogene, 33
Aldrich, Charles H., 40
Aldrich, Harriet L. 8
Aldrich, Louise E., 43
Aldrich, Rebecca B., 9
Aldrich, Melzer N., 9
Aldrich, Myron H., 9
Aldrich, P. M., 43
Allen, Emma C., 23
Allen, George E., 40
Allerton, Florence, 48
Allerton, Ransom, 48
Allerton, Sanford, 8
Allyn, Christopher, 11
Allyn, Henry, 11
Allyn, Mr., 11
Amerman, Albert, 8
Ames, William, 34
Anderson, Julia E., 38
Andrews, Fanny, 25
Angell, J., 51
Angell, Nathan, 55
Anscomb, Susan, 42
Antisdale, J. Franklin, 28
Ardell, Sara P., 39
Arms, Almira, 6, 7
Arms, Charles, 16
Arms, Elizabeth, 16
Arms, Morris, 6, 7
Arnold, Jane E., 46
Arzberger, Thomas, 46
Arzberger, William, 46

Atkinson, Mrs. 25
Atkinson, Thomas, 34
Atwood, George A., 29
Austen, Nathan L., 32
Austin, Ferdando, 26
Austin, James, 7
Austin, James P., 14
Avery, Emma J., 25
Babcock, Charles, 37
Babcock, Edward H., 15
Babcock, Charles, 37
Babcock, Phebe, 26
Bacus, Ella A., 54
Bagley, James, 44
Bailey, Benjamin, 21
Bailey, Evangelia, 21
Baker, Charles, 29
Baker, Joshua,(Mrs), 22
Baker, Leroy, 29
Baker, Marcus, 42
Baldwin, Amanda, 34
Baldwin, Harry, 34
Baldwin, Mrs., 18
Baldwin, William H., 34
Baltzell, Mr., 21
Barclay, Abram, 31
Barclay, Cephese, 31
Barclay, H., 18
Barhite, Alma, 12
Barnard, Frances, 21
Barnhart, Hattie L., 23
Barral, Charles Henry, 48
Barral, Henry, 48
Barral, Magdalena, 48
Barrow, Orrin, 39
Bartle, James P. 53, 54
Bartle, Louisa B., 54
Barton, Alice M., 42
Barton, Elihu, 16
Barton, Isaac, 42
Barton, Martha, 16
Barton, Mary, 36
Bassett, H. Dwight, 45
Batershall, Walton W., 9
Battershall, Anna Davidson, 47
Battershall, Walton W., 47
Baxter, Alice, 36
Baxter, Orselah, 51
Baxter, Witter J., 36

57

Beach, Gertie, 48
Beadle, George S., 50
Beals, Anna Augusta, 30
Beals, Ira, 30
Beam, Andrew J., 29
Bean, Michael, 37
Beaumont, A. L., 36
Beckwith, Eliza J., 14
Beckwith, T. Tobias, 31
Beebe, William W., 31
Beiler, Henry, 7
Bell, Emma G., 9
Bell, Henry, 47
Bell, Samuel B., 33
Bellinger, William, 38
Bellinger, Samuel, 38
Bellows, Tryphena H., 6
Benham, Eli, 33
Bennett, Charles, 15
Bennett, J. Yates, 6
Bennett, Mariette G., 6
Bennett, Martha Jane, 24
Bennett, Susan Lucena, 24
Bentley, George H., 45
Berns, Henry, 51
Berns, Mary, 51
Berry, Charles, 33
Beswick, Charles A., 52
Bidwell, D. D., 44
Bigelow, Charles, 50
Bigelow, Libbie, 50
Billings, Allyn B., 12
Bircher, M. (Mrs), 39
Birdsall, J., 22
Birdsall, Samuel, 32
Bishop, Phebe Jane, 15
Blackmar, Belcher, 8
Blackmar, Frank, 9
Blackmar, Horace, 8
Blakeman, Demas, 40
Blakesley, M. P., 41
Blanden, J. S., 45
Blinn, George W. W., 41
Bliss, Calvin H., 49
Bliss, Louisa T., 49
Bloomer, A. S., 50
Bloomer, Clintie M. 50
Bloomer, Nellie, 50
Bloomer, S. M., 50
Bloomer, Samuel, 50
Bockover, George E., 27
Bogardus, E., 50

Bolls, F. A., 16
Bolster, Dwight A., 16
Bonacker, B., 38
Bonacker, Eva, 38
Borrodaile, C. R., 7
Borrodaile, Emma, 7
Bortles, Fannie E., 43
Bostwick, Victor M., 13
Bosworth, N., 42
Bottom, Mary, 53
Bottum, Cornie, 13
Bottum, E. W., 13
Bourne, John H., 44
Bourne, Robert. 44
Bown, (Bowen?), C. L., 35
Bowen. See Bown
Box, Sarah, 25
Box, George, 25
Boyd, James A. (Mrs.), 49
Boyd, John, 35
Boyd, Kate, 35
Boyd, Millard, 33
Boyd, James A. (Mrs), 49
Boyer, Lydia, 14
Boynton, J. S., 32
Boynton, John, 33
Boyton, L. S., 32
Braden, Abram S., 52
Bradley, Benjamin J., 21
Bradley, Eliza, 21
Bradley, John, 27
Bradley, Luanna L., 27
Bradt, Cornelia, 6
Brant, Peter, 41
Brayton, B. B., 33
Brewster, Cornelius, 46
Brower, Edward R., 15
Brown, Emma, 23
Brown, Milton S., 9
Brown, Andrew J., 13
Brown, Susan Allyn, 11
Brown, Ella F., 28
Brown, Julia, 53
Brownell, John M., 39, 49
Brownell, John N., (Mrs), 22
Brownell, Willis, 40
Brundage, Ann, 38
Brundage, Alvah, 38
Brundage, Margaret Ann, 389
Bryant, Vietta V., 16
Bryant, James T., 20
Bryant, Albert A., 17

Bryant, Calvin W., 40
Bryant, James T., 20
Bryant, William S., 9
Buck, D. D., 6, 8, 10
Buck, Philena, 10
Buck, Rev., 5
Buell, M. D. L., 53
Buerman, John, 15
Buerman, Sarah, 15
Bullard, Hamilton, 41
Bullard, Sarah, 41
Bump, Emogene, 34
Bump, Helen A., 24
Burgdorf, Rev., 5
Burgdorf, J. C. 7, 8, 9, 10, 11, 12, 13, 15, 18, 19, 24, 26, 28, 29, 32, 45, 54
Burgdorf, Martia I., 54
Burgess, Clara, 29
Burgess, Mary J., 18
Burgess, James (Mrs), 43
Burgess, W. W., 27
Burgett, Frankie S., 45
Burleigh, William, 10
Burnett, James, 25
Burnett, Mary, 35
Bush, Emogene F., 28
Butler, Jonathan, 14
Butler, Libbie A., 8
Butterfield, Rebecca S., 53
Button, Alexandria, 12
Button, Pamela, 12
Button, Richard, 22
Butts, Albert, 44
Buys, Williams, 18
Cady, Jerry, 17
Cady, Elias, 37
Cady, Fanny, 17
Cady, George, 37
Calhoun, Sanford P., 40
Campbell, Daniel (Mrs), 31
Campbell, Dr., 22
Campbell, James S., 14
Carey, Doc., 34
Carey, John T., 20
Carlisle, Martha A., 35
Cartman, Thomas, 14
Cary, Lyman, 28
Case, Etta, 25
Case, Frank, 12
Case, Gamaliel, 12
Case, John, 5

Chadwick, Ezra (Mrs), 48
Champlin, William, 13
Champlin, Florence, 13
Chapman, Frank W., 10
Chapman, J., 18
Chase, Clark S., 45
Chase, Durfee, 30
Chase, Louis M., 45
Chipman, A. H., 30
Chittenden, Orville, 6
Clark, Aaron, 6
Clark, Myron E., 14
Clark, Nettie A., 26
Clarke, Charles H., 24
Clarke, Joseph, 47
Claven, Nellie J., 50
Clemons, Fannie L., 48
Coane, Judida, 5
Cobb, Charlotte, 40
Cochran, J. E. (Mrs), 35
Colburn, John F, 48
Cole, Alice, 29
Cole, Alice A., 29
Cole, Cassie, 7
Cole, Lucius, 24
Cole, Hannah, 10
Cole, Samuel, 44
Cole, William W., 27
Collins, Frank, 13
Collins, Jeffery, 46
Collins, Stephen, 46
Collins, T. W., 13
Colvin, William P. M., 26
Colwell, Murray, 10
Combs, Amelia L., 32
Cone, Sarah A., 44
Congdon, Cynthia, 49
Cook, Eliza, 32
Cooley, E., 16
Cornell, J. A. H., 14
Corning, Joseph W., 22
Cornwall, John J., 10
Corwin, Nancy, 51
Cory, Charles, 22
Covell, Oren B., 52
Covert, Humphrey W., 33
Cox, A. C., 19
Cox, Mary L., 47
Crafts A. P., 27
Crafts, Emily A., 27
Craggs, Richard, 55
Cragin, Andrew, 53

Cramer, David S., 33
Cramer, Fannie M., 15
Cramer, George, 15
Crane, Ella C., 29
Crego, Lorena, 37
Cressy, Noah, 42
Croft, David, 5
Crommerr, Florine J., 29
Crommett, M. Louisa, 5
Cromwell, N. (Mrs), 50
Cronise, Carrie, J., 43
Cronise, Ella, 9
Cronise, Estelle M., 19
Cronk, Ida B., 8
Cronk, L. W., 8
Crosby, Lizzie O., 51
Crothers, Mary, 16
Crothers, Oliver, 16
Cuddeback, Deborah, 47
Culver, George A., 23
Culver, Alethia Estelle, 8
Culver, Helen M., 23
Culver, Norman, 8, 12
Culver, Stephen, 46
Cummings, Florence L., 52
Currey, Burtiss, 26
Curtis, James H., 42
Curtiss, J. Myron, 53
Cuyler, George W., 31, 42
Cuyler, Georgianna, 31
Cuyler, Samuel C., 32
Czerny, Josi A., 49
Czerny, Magdalena, 49
Daboll, Henry H., 25
Daggett, John, 8, 20
Danford, Orrin, 10
Daniels, Hosea, 46
Darby, Chauncey, 25
Darling, Eli, 25
Davenport, Samuel, 18
Davidson, Isaac, 16
Davis, Benjamin (Mrs), 31
Davison Anna M., 9
DeBrine, James, 14
DeBrine, Jennie, 14
Decay, Morris (Mrs), 10
DeGraff, William M., 10
Deitz, Elizabeth, 39
Delevan, Wealthy, 16
Deming, Sarah Ann., 41
Dempsey, Milton, 43
Denier, Libbie, 53

Dennison, John M., 40
Denny, John, 33
Depew, Harriet H., 29
Deright, Herman, 6, 7
DeRight, Widow, 37
DeVolder, Mary, 14
Dickenson, Joseph, 43
Dickenson, Lydia, 43
Dickie, William, 41
Dickinson, Mary Janet, 25
Diddy, Laura A., 48
Diets, Christine, 18
Dillenback, John, 22
Dodd, Henry, 16
Dodd, John, 13
Doty, Helen E., 53
Douglass, Stephen P. W., 49
Dowd, J. H., 7
Drake, Benson C., 8
Drake, Harry, 12
Drake, John M., 42
Drake, Mary C., 8
Drake, N. G, 45
Drake, R. S., 41
Drake, Sarah A, 41
Dratt, Abram, 34
Drowne, Charles, 43
Dubois, Abraham, A., 53
Dubois, Mary, 53
Dubois, William C., 53
Dunning, John, 52
Dunning, R., 15
Dunning, Richard, 16
Durfee, Lemuel, 21
Dutcher, John, 38
Dyson, John, 15
Eastman, Hattie, 31
Eastman, O., 31
Eaton, H., 25
Eaton, H. A., 41
Eaton, Horace, 27
Eddy, Alice E., 15
Edmondston, William, 29
Eggleston, Dr., 7
Eggleston, Mehetable, 32
Eggleston, Thomas, 32
Elliott, Charles G., 52
Ellis, B. V., 34
Ellis, Lydia, 34
Ellsworth, Ammi, 24
Ellsworth, Levi 25
Elmendorf, Eugene, 26

Ely, M. G., 40
Ely, Sophia, 40
Ely, William, 40
Ernst, Abby, 40
Ernst, Eliza Agnes, 36, 40
Ernst, George, 36, 40
Ernst, Henry, 40
Espenscheid, Elizabeth, 51
Evans, Cornelia M., 17
Evans, Dora Belle, 17
Evans, Hattie May, 17
Evans, Ludelia, 16
Evans, Monroe, 17
Everett, George, H., 30
Everett, Rueben T., 30
Exner, Mrs., 46
Fahnstock, Louisa, 23
Fahy, Mr. 39
Fairchild, Nancy, 50
Feller, Arthur D., 5
Feller, Philip I., 36
Feller, Victor, 36
Fellers, Mary, 17
Fellers, Robert, 17
Felshaw, Samuel, 7
Fenster, N. J., 53
Field, Willard M., 23
Filkins, Francis M., 32
Fillenham, Lottie E., 53
Fillmore, Ella J., 29
Finley, Jay R., 29
Fisher, M. A., 30
Fisk, James C., 35
Fiske, Judson, 17
Fleming, Catharine M., 43
Fleming, William, 43
Flynn, Thomas, 50
Folwell, W. R., 45
Fonda, Giles, 51
Fonda, Sarah E., 18
Ford, Belle, 54
Ford, James D., 28
Foree, Alice P., 20
Forte, Clara May, 41
Forte, Emily E., 41
Forte, Irving C., 41
Forte, Lucy N., 23
Foster, Baily, 26
Foster, Cullen, 14
Foster, Dewitt P., 26
Foster, Nellie M., 11
Fowler, George, 48

Fowler, William, 48
Frear, Charles, 6
Frear, Nellie, 15
Frear, William S. L., 54
Freeman, A. R., 19
Freeman, Nathaniel, 22
Freeman, S. Alden, 23
French, Laura A., 45
French, Mary, 7
Fuchs, Felizidas, 35
Fuller, Addison, 43
Fuller, Kittie L., 52
Fulton, Nancy, 24
Fulton, Robert, 24
Gardner, Edgar, 38
Gardner, Hale, 35
Gardner, Leman, 27
Garlick, Henry, 33
Garlick, Sally, 33
Garlock, George, 11
Garlock, Matilda, 11
Garlock, Samuel C., 11
Garratt, Mary E., 30
Garret, B., 18
Garret, Helen, 18
Garrison, Martin, 14
Gates, Alice, 32
Gates, William F., 28
Gauthner, Frederick, Jr., 18
Genung, Mary D., 42
German, Smith, 44
Gibbard, Isaac, 11
Gibbs, Benega, 16
Gibbs, Manle, 18
Gibbs, Martin, 18
Gibbs, Sally, 16
Gibbs, W., 23
Gilkey, Mary, 28
Gilmore, James T., 50
Goldsmith, Lydia, 54
Goodsell, Allen, 13
Goodwin, Robert E., 46
Gordon, Mollie, E., 44
Goseline, Joseph M., 40
Gothorpe, Libbie, 9
Grace, Henry, 36
Grady, B. O., 39
Gramke, J. 7
Gramke, Mary, 7
Grandin, Phebe, 23
Grandin, William L., 23
Graves, John, 25

Graves, John B., 54
Graves, Mrs., 54
Gray, John, 28
Gray, Mary, 28
Green, Max G., 43
Green, T. R., 35
Grimes, Martin E. 45
Grimes, Viola, 45
Grimm, Henry, 36, 38
Grimm, Julia, 38
Grimm, Lewis, 38
Griswold, Aaron, 27
Griswold, L., 48
Griswold, William H., 48
Gross, Alex, 25
Gunnison, Howell Bidwell, 44
Gunnison, Sarah B., 44
Gunnison, William B., 44
Hadden, J. L., 18
Haight, Emma, 8
Haight, John, 50
Haight, Orlando, 46
Hall, Olney, 26
Halley, E., 31
Hance, Benjamin, 48
Hance, Samuel, 48
Hanson, Ellen, 15
Harden, Hannah, 25
Harding, Helen, 19
Harding, James, 13
Harding, William, 9
Harkness, Betsey, 53
Harman, Dollie, 18
Harmon, Jennie, 13
Harness, Francis G., 28
Harris, J. M., 41
Harris, John, 30
Harris, Richard, 24
Harter, J. H., 27
Hartman, Daniel L.
Hawley, Mary A., 31
Haynes, Jerome C., 54
Hazen, Nelson (Mrs), 21
Heath, Evaline, 27
Heath, Jennie E., 30
Hicks, Carrie, 5
Hicks, Gardner, 44
Hicks, George, 9
Hicks, Rebecca, 44
Hickson, Carrie, 54
Higgins, Dell A., 22
Higgins, Erasmus H., 5

Hill, Anthony, 39
Hill, Benjamin (Mrs.), 49
Hill, Caroline, 39
Hill, Ella A., 28
Hill, Eunice E., 39
Hill, Helen, 29
Hill, Kate, 17
Hill, M. O., 51
Hill, Parley, 28
Hill, Peter, 39
Hill, Pliny, 19
Hill, Riley, 23
Hill, Susie A., 28
Hill, William H., 39
Hinton, L., 51
Hislop, John G., 31
Hislop, William G., 38
Hoag, Sally F., 33
Hoag, Wilson, 33
Hodge, James, 21
Hodskin, E. L., 8
Hoetzel, Julia A., 49
Hogoboom, R., 22
Hollenbeck, Casper, 46
Hollenbeck, Lucy, 46
Holley, Julia K., 39
Hollister, Marvin, 36
Hollister, Sarah, 36
Holmes, Anna, 34
Homewood, John, 38
Hooper, Carrie, 30
Hooper, Spencer, 29
Hopkins, A. J., 45
Hopkins, Bridget, 41
Hopkins, Eunice, 55
Hopkins, James, 7
Hopkins, Murganzy, 53
Hopkins, William. 55
Horn, A., 9
Hornbeck. George E., 28
Hornbeck, Lurinda L., 19
Horton, Benjamin, 21
Hosford, Luther C., 42
Hough, Nellie, 40
Hough, S. Porter, 8
Hough, W. W., 40
Houser, Eliza, 39
Howard, Lucy Ann, 35
Howe, Etta, 25
Howe, Rose A., 42
Hoyt, Mary A., 33
Hudson, Charles, 46

Hudson, T. B., 47
Hughson, Jeremiah, 13
Hulbert, Leroy, 48
Hulett, S. P., 13
Hunt, Alice, 17
Hunter, Ellen, 25
Huntoon, Charles, 53
Hurley, Mary, 29
Husted, Emma E., 24
Ingersoll, Edward, 19
Ireland, J., 7
Ireland, T., 17
Irish, Agnes R., 19
Irish, Charles G., 19
Ives, Helen S., 20
Ives, John M., 41
Jackson, Albert E., 20
Jackson, Caroline, 20,
Jackson, Cyrus, 47
Jackson, James, 33,
Jackson, Jane, 47
Jackson, Stillman, 33
Jagger, Milton C., 12
James, L. R., 10
Jameson, Charles H., 23
Jepson, Eli, 52
Jeremiah, Louise, 21
Jerome, Roswell H., 32
Johnson, Alice, 15
Johnson, David, 45
Johnson, Luke C., 25
Johnson, Mary, 24
Johnson, MattieE., 45,
Johnson, Nancy, 43
Johnson, S. P., 7
Johnson, William, 26
Jolley, Rev., 31
Jones, A. T., 24
Jones, Allen, 53
Jones, Andrew B., 27
Jones, Emily L., 24
Joslyn, Thankful, 36
Keller, William H., 8
Kelley, C. P., 20
Kelly, E. W., 48
Kelley, Emily, 20
Kelley, George, 20
Kelley, Hannah H., 20
Kelley, J. G. (Mrs), 7
Kelsey, Jeanette, 11
Kennedy, A., 19
Kennedy, Jennie, 19

Kent, Frank O., 52
Kenyon, George Z. T., 15
Kenyon, M. M., 54
Kesson, Thomas, 18
Ketchum, Leander S., 14
King, Adelbert, 37
King, Alonzo H., 15
King, Calvin, 21
Kipp, Huldy, 37
Kipp, J. H., 37
Kirby, Anna, 47
Knapp, Eliza, 10
Knapp, Mable, 10
Knapp, Nathan, 10
Knapp, Simeon, 42
Knight, David, 24
Knoblock, John, 33
Knox, Charles, 44
Knox, Edward, 30
Knox, John, 22
Knox, Lucinda, 30
Koester, Charles, 52
Krum, Adella O., 9
Krum, John S., 9
Krum, Louisa, 11
Krum, S., 14, 31
Ladue, O. T., 26
Lake, Stepehn, 35
Lamoreaux, Aaron D., 19
Lamoreaux, Flora, 27
Lampman, Jude, 42
Landon, E. B. S., 5
Landon, Orrin, 27
Lane, Electa, 29
Langdon, Wilson A., 19
Langworthy, Charles I., 28
Lanridge, Martin, 17
Lape, Jesse, 43
Lape, Lemuel, 43
Lapham, John, 32
Lapham, Porter, 32
Latimer, Charles W., 54
Laubenheimer, Louis, 14
Lawrence, Elizabeth, 29
Lawrence, Walter, 29
Lay, Lucia H., 14
Lay, Robert S., 14
Layton, Charles S., 34
Layton, Daniel, 34
Layton, Frank, 32
Layton, Henrietta, J., 34
Lazenby, Maggie, 36

Leach, Anson O., 36
Leach, Charles H., 36
Leach, Elizabwth G., 36
Leach, H. J., 36
Leach, J. (Mrs.), 26
Leach, John H., 34
Leach, Ruth A., 36
Leach, Ruth Ann, 36
Leighton, J., 27
Lemunion, Carrie E., 28
Leroy, Rose, 28
Lester, W. H., 40
Lewis, Frank E., 39
Lewis, G. L., 39
Lienhart, Henry, 45
Lilly, A. H., 11, 12
Lincoln, Charles, 50
Littebrant, Christina, 12
Lord, Francis J., 11
Lord, Horace B., 28
Lord, Ichabod, 11
Loveland, Levi A., 6
Lovett, Joseph C., 41
Lummis, Georgiana, 42
Lund, Robert, 33
Lusk, Ella D., 9
Lusk, Minnie, 9
Lusk, R. Almon, 9
Lux, B. (Mrs), 40
Lux, Mary, 49
Lyman, A., 51
Lyman, Abel, 44
Lynch, Mary, 50
Lyons, Peter, 33
Lyre, J., 52
Maine, Nettie A., 15
Maines, Deborah, 47
Malcomb, Elizabeth, 46
Male, Francis, 23
Mann, Owen, 54
Manning, William, 29, 30, 32, 45, 48, 54
Mansfield, Kate, 37
Marsh, Charles E., 24
Marsh, George F., 37
Martin, Abraham, 34
Martin, Ella, 50
Martin, Eliza McMannus, 24
Martin, Hiram, 24
Martin, Mary, 19
Martin, Thomas, 19
Mason, G. H. (Mrs), 9

Mastin, Abel M., 39
Mastin, Stephen H., 39
Mayer, Eve A., 7
Mayer, H. F. C., 7
Mayer, Nettie, 7
McClellan, George R., 38
McClellan, Ruba E., 30
McCollum, Jessie, 9
McCorkle, W. A., 9
McFarland, Albert G., 12
McGinnis, John E., 23
McGonigal, Charles, 38
McGonigal, Ida, 38
McGregor, P., 38
McIntosh, Mary A., 33
McIntyre, Ann B., 24
McIntyre, S. B., 24
McLean, J. B., 16
McLouth, Charles, 31
McMath, William, 51
McNeil, James, 32
Meachem, Melvin, 7
Mead, Julia, 49
Mead, T. G., 49
Meade, Baron A., 22
Meeker, Benjamin S., 28
MeMarse, Eli, 33
Merrill, Lucy T., 52
Mesick, John, 12
Messenger, Edward, 39
Messenger, Ida, 51
Messenger, William C., 39
Metz, Fred K., 40
Metz, William Frederick, 40
Miles, Erastus, 46
Miles, Rev., 13
Miller, Addie, 26
Miller, Ann, 25
Miller, Ann H., 26
Miller, Charles, 32
Miller, Frederick, 28
Miller, James H., 32
Miller, Samuel, 32
Millerd, George F., 34
Mills, Charles, 17
Mills, William C., 22
Miln, Edward, 28
Miln, George, 34
Miner, Catherine, 35
Miner, D. N., 45
Miner, Minerva M., 43
Miner, Vila B., 45

Miner, William B., 35
Mirick, Albertine, 26
Mirick, Ira, 26
Mirrick, S. H., 22
Mitchell, Jacob (Mrs.), 34
Moffit, Jeduthan, 17
Moffit, Nancy, 17
Montgomery, George W., 15
Montrose, M. Augusta, 51
Moore, Ann, 38
Moore, Martha H., 53
Moore, Robert N., 24
Moore, William L., 48
Moran, Patrick, 55
Morely, Lucy Louisa, 49
Morely, Samuel S., 49
Morgan, Sally, 27
Morse, William B., 12
Mosher, Hugh S., 22
Moule, Jonathan, 50
Mulligan, Mrs., 46
Munford, Mary E., 12
Munson, Mary Ann, 26
Murray, John, 50
Neale, Moses, 21
Neiderlander, Sally N., 11
Nellis, P. E., 30
Newbury, Walter S., 25
Newman, George Alonzo, 25
Newport, Calvin, 45
Newport, Titus, 45
Newton, Alonzo, 54
Newton, John R., 31
Nicholay, William H, 16
Nichols, Thomas, 47
Nickerson, Wakeman T., 47
Niderer, Anton, 35
Norris, B. F., 19
North, Elias, 10
North, H. H., 37
North, Nelson G., 37
Novess, Henry (Mrs), 54
O'Byne, John, 54
Odell, Francisca G., 15
O'Dell, Esbon, 30
O'Dell, Jesse B., 12
Odell, Susan, 12
Olcox, Mrs., 17
Olmstead, S. L., 18
Onderkonk, Harriet Celia, 10
Ostrander, Freeman, 14
Ostrander, O. S., 43

Ottman, Emma J., 7
Otto, Mary R., 51
Paddock, George W., 18
Padget, Francis A, 13
Padget, Thomas, 13
Page, Anna L, 45
Page, W. F., 45
Palmer, Eva E., 29
Palmeter, Eliza, 18
Pane, William, 29
Pardee, A. (Mrs.), 40
Parker, Dr., 8
Parker, Electa, 24
Parker, Joseph C., 28
Parker, Mary, 51
Parks, Effie, 26
Parks, M. E., 19
Partridge, James, 29
Partidge, William A., 47
Paton, William, 36
Patten, James W., 12
Patten, Julius C., 12
Patten, Narcissa, 12
Patterson, Charles, 34
Pease, Dwight A., 7
Peckham, J. Coggeshall, 30
Peer, David, 36
Pellys, Myron, 39
Peppino, S. S., 42
Percy, Thomas, 17
Perrin, Edgar, 44
Perrine, George W., 38
Petrie, Joseph C., 26
Pettengill, Rev., 9
Pettys, Matthew, 13
Philips, Adelia, 50
Pierce, Ann, 23
Pierce, G. R., 7, 19
Pierce, J., 17
Pierce, J. R., 17
Pierce, Jane, 15
Pierce, Nettie, 31
Pierce, Julia A., 31
Pierson, Samuel A., 51
Pierce, William, 15, 23
Piggot, W., 11
Pitcher, Freelove, 9
Pitcher, Jacob, 9
Plumb, Daniel, 48
Pollard, Rev., 15
Pollock, James, 50
Pomeroy, Emma C., 46

Porter, Jennie, 34
Posse, Thomas, 42
Post, Anna, 37
Post, Emma J., 27
Post, Henry, 27
Post, William E., 11
Potter, A. C., 25
Potter, Albert H., 44
Powell, Charles E., 28
Power, William A., 45
Powers, Susan, 49
Prescott, Joel, 21
Prescott, Joel H., 21
Prescott, Joel Henry, 19
Price, A. J. (Mrs.) 47
Prince, Cyrus D., 36
Pritchard, Hannah, 45
Proseus, John (Mrs), 41
Pullman, Darius, 54
Pullman, Louisa, 54
Pulver, Jacob, 23
Pulver, John (Mrs), 19, 20
Pulver, Levi, 43
Pulver, Lucia, 23
Pulver, Wandall, 25
Raddar, Eliza, 47
Randolph, M., 10
Randolph, Rev., 10
Ray, Edward T., 52, 53
Ray, Henry, 41
Ray, William R., 41
Reaves, J. H., 29
Redner, P., 51
Reed, Sarah, 22
Reed, Harvey Wilson, 23
Reed, Lucy, 25
Reed, E. D., 24
Reed, Sophia, 24
Reed, Charles H., 33
Reed, Sarah A., 23
Reed, Laura L., 36
Reed, Emma, 33
Reeves, Abiah H., 44
Reeves, James, 17
Reeves, Paul, 17
Reeves, Sarah, 17
Reeves, Zebulon, 44
Rew, E. B., 44
Reynold, Clark, 15
Reynold, Jane, 15
Reynolds, Randolph, 36
Reynolds, Robert, 37

Reynolds, Samuel S., 18
Reynolds, Silas, 39
Rhumbolt, James, 47
Rice, Myron, 23
Rice, Austin, 26
Rice, Elmira E., 49
Rice, James, 49
Rice, Josiah, 23
Richards, Katie, 29
Richardson, Sophia A., 32
Ridley, Eva, 10
Ridley, Elihu, 11
Ridley, Mr., 11
Rihn, Peter, 54
Rinkel, Emma, 54
Rinkel, Eva, 49, 51, 54
Rinkel, Michael, 49, 51, 54
Rinkel, William H., 49
Roberts, Carrie S., 38
Roberts, H. N., 38
Robinson, George E., 25
Robinson, Hattie, 50
Robinson, M. E., 19
Robinson, J. C., 15
Robinson, Minard, 29
Robinson, Rowland, 14
Robinson, Thomas, 18
Robinson, Susan, 37
Robinson, William H., 48
Rockfeller, Libbie, 10
Rodwell, Fanny, 47
Rogers, Harriet H., 39
Rogers, Lucy M., 52
Rogers, Thomas, 39
Rose, Antoinette, 29
Rose, L. L., 47
Rose, Nellie, 47
Ross, Charles, 54
Rowe, Ella M., 29
Rowe, Sarah, 11
Royce, John, 17
Roys, Charles H., 39
Roys, E. Joseph, 32
Roys, John C., 34
Rudd, Rev., 13
Runyon, Kittie A., 8
Runyon, L., 37
Runyon, W. W., 8, 27, 35, 37, 43, 52, 53
Rutherford, Mary E., 35
Ryckman, David, 34
Ryckman, Jennie, 34

Ryder, Catharine, 34
Ryder, Willie, 34
Sabine, D. J., 14
Saddler, C. A., 16
Sadler, Phebe, 16
Sanford. David, 37
Sanford, David P. (Mrs), 21
Sanford, George Ray, 47
Sanford, George W., 40
Sanford, Georgia May, 45
Sanford, James M., 26
Sanford, Luther, 46
Sanford, Mary, 45, 47
Sanford, Ruth, 46
Sanford, S. W., 47
Sanford, Smith W., 45
Saunders, Joseph, 48
Saunders, Sarah, 48
Sayles, Amelia Ann, 10
Sayles, Manley, 10
Seargeant, George, 13
Searle, Burton, 33
See, Revilo M., 27
Seeley, Albert, 29
Seeley, James, 37
Sergeant, Hannah, 49
Sewall, A. C, 20, 22, 31, 33, 40, 51
Sewall, G. P., 20
Sewell, Rev., 19
Seymour, Emma, 16
Shannon, Mary E., 37
Shaver, George, 44
Shaver, Lena, 44
Shaw, P. K., 37
Sahaw, Richard, 37
Shaw, William (Mrs), 35
Sheffield, Tabitha, 32
Shepard, Mrs., 33
Sherman, D. A., 13
Sherman, Edward, 50
Sherman, Humphrey, 48
Sherman, Samuel Albert, 11
Sherman, W. O., 13
Sherman, William, 49
Shindler, John, 46
Shoales, Benjamin, 31
Shockly, Ellen, 51
Short, Avis G., 31
Short, Chester F., 18
Short, Lena, 11
Short, Mattie, 31

Short, Nancy, 33
Short, Rev., 52
Short, Seneca, 48
Short, S. S., 33
Short, Seymour S., 33
Shufelt, Jane E., 49
Shufelt, John J., 49
Shulte, Henry, 5
Shumway, Catherine, 5
Shumway, G. R. H., 11
Shurtleff, A. H., 51
Sibbet, Jonathan, 35
Sibett, Walter A., 36
Simons, Harriet M., 43
Simons, Peter, 43
Simpson, James, 32
Simpson, John, 34
Simpson, Mary, 32
Skinner, Elizabeth, 51
Skinner, S. H. (Mrs), 26
Skinner, Sarah H., 28
Skinner, Warren, 51
Skuse, Philetus M., 8
Sloan, Ada A., 52
Sloan, Anderson G., 52
Sloan, W. H., 31, 52
Smith, Nellie C., 22
Smith, A., (Mrs), 25
Smith, A. P., 23
Smith, Almyra, 16
Smith, Anna, 27
Smith, Caleb, 34
Smith, Carrie, 30
Smith, Charles, 37 41
Smith, Daniel G., 24
Smith, E. P., 14, 16
Smith, Ellen, 44
Smith, Eugene, , 44
Smith, Gurdon T., 39
Smith, Henry, 37
Smith, J. D., 24
Smith, John J., 43
Smith, John L., 11
Smith, Mabel, 44
Smith, Maria, , 46
Smith, Mary, 51
Smith, Melissa, 39
Smith, Morgan L., 29
Smith, P. V. N., 46
Smith, Rhoda, 7
Smith, Sarah M., 50
Smith, Thomas, 51

Smith, William, 29
Smith, Z. W., 21
Snyder, Amos, 37
Snyder, Mary Ann, 30
Snyder, Jacob L., 14
Snyder, George S., 30, 43
Snyder, Samuel, 28
Snyder, Stephen, 53
Sober, John Albert, 29
Sober, Jonathan, 29
Sober, Mary, 29
Souden, John, 33
Sours, John, 17
Southard, M. E., 35
Southard, N. D., 35
Southard, Nathan D., 35
Southwick, Henry W., 38
Soverhill Gardner M., 20
Spaulding, W. J., 16
Spencer, William, 36
Spier, William Elbert, 25
Spink, John, 14
Spinks, J., 8, 10
Spinks, John, 5
Spoor, Ella, 6
Spoor, J. W., 6
Sproull, R. D., 31
St John, Anna P., 11
St John, Charles G., 11
St John, Charles R., 5
St Clair, George, 42
Stack, Jacob, 25
Stafford, Alice J., 23
Stafford. J. H., 23
Stafford, Mott, 38
Stafford, Phebe, 38
Stanton, George T., 30
Stark, James, 24
Steadman, Ella, 32
Stearns, A. H., 30
Stearns, Madison L., 11.
Stebbins, Carles, 10
Stebbins, C. A., 53
Stebbins, Ellen M., 10
Stebbins, Josephus, 53
Steeley, J. T., 1
Stephenson, Isaac, 9
Stevens, Aaron C., 52
Stevens, Kate E., 40
Stever, Frances, 5
Stever, Cleon. E., 36
Stever, Francis, 5

Stever, Jacob E., 36
Stever, Rebecca J., 36
Steverson, J. A., 52
Stone, Emanuel, 50
Stone, S. D. (Mrs), 29
Stonebridge, John, 45
Stonebridge, Spencer Mead, 45
Strickland, Martha, 34
Strickland, Samuel, 34
Strong, Nathan R., 16
Stroud, Frank H., 16
Stuart, John, 22
Sturges, Chester S., 34
Sturgess, William, 13
Sunderlin, Emsley C., 6
Supple, Miss, 26
Sutter, Lana, 28
Sutton, Hattie, 18
Swales, John, 14
Swales, George, 14
Swales, William, 7
Sweet, D. B., 26
Sweet, Julia Ann, 26
Sweet, Sidney S., 51
Sweeting, Anna Eliza, 34
Taber, Lewis E., 50
Tallmadge, Charles E., 30
Tanner, Mary L., 38
Tassell, Mary, 52
Tater, Cyrus, A., 18
Taylor, Daniel E., 9
Taylor, George B., 9
Taylor, George Z., 47
Taylor, Solon, 5
Teller, Kate, 35
Teller, William H., 35
Tenley, Joseph, 20
Terbush, Amanda, 26
Terry, Amelia, 53
Thayer, A. A., 23
Thomas, Byron, 22
Thomas, R., 12
Thomas, Rodman, 12
Thompson, Hiram, 39
Tiffany, Catharine R., 46
Tiffany, Edwin, 46
Tilden, Libbie M., 52
Tillotson, Elizabeth, 21
Tingue, John, 7
Tinney, Salem G., 31
Titus, Anson S, Jr., 52
Titus, Carrie A. 53

Todd, Asahel, 20
Todd, Ella, 22
Tonsworth, James, 19
Townsend, Stephen, 24
Tramper, Ella, 38
Tramper, J. E., 38
Travice, Job, 31
Travice, Phebe A., 31
Tryon, Emma, 21
Tryon, William, 21
Tucker, Alice, 27
Tucker, Pomeroy, 27
Tucker, William L, 23
Tufts, M. J. Elam, 42
Turner, Addison, 43
Turner, Addison (Mrs), 34
Tyler, Adeliza, 14
Van Duzen, Emma, 10
Van Ostrand, Nancy, 42
VanAlstine, Carrie, 30
VanAlstyne, G., 9, 12
VanAlstyne, George, 11, 18, 19
VanAmburgh, Henry C., 53
VanAuken, Abram, 17
VanAuken, Charles, 17
VanBenschoten, Richard, 50
VanBuren, D. L., 7
Vandeberg, Allie Bell, 45
Vandeburg, James W, 45,
Vandeberg, Peter, 25
Vandeberg, Rebecca, 25
Vanderbilt, A. H. 36
Vanderbilt, Abram, 36
Vanderbilt, Julia Ann, 36
Vanderbilt, N. T., 36
Vanderhoof, Allen, 16
Vanderhoof, Flora D., 16
Vanderpool, J. G., 24
Vanderpool, L., 24
Vandusen, Anna L., 53
Vandusen, Emma P., 53
Vandusen, J. P., 53
Vandusen, Walter, 22
VanDyck, Louis, 26
VanDyne, Charles H., 54
VanDyne, Henry, 51
VanGorder, Charlotte, 6
VanInwagon, Emma Maria, 11
VanSlyck, P., 30
VanVrocklin, Sylvester, 8
VanWickle, Minerva, 24
Vary, Jay S., 45

Veeder, Simon H., 50
Vibbard, Carrie, 31
Vorhees, James, 27
Vosburg, Lottie, 5
Vosburgh, John, 35
Vosburgh, Mary, 35
Wader, J. A., 9
Wadsworth, Craig, 30
Wadsworth, James S., 30
Wake, Ella M., 341
Wake, John, 31
Wakeman, Catherine, 5
Walbridge, Arthur D., 53
Walbridge, Maria, 53
Walbridge, S. D., 53
Walhizer, Andrew, 51
Walker, Robert, 27
Wallace, H. H., 9
Wallace, Samuel, 9
Walrath, Hannah, 38
Walrath, Henry, 38
Walton, Charles, 46
walton, George William, 46
Walton, Thomas, 30
Walton, William, 30
Ward, Ellen, 52
Ward, Eustatia, 9
Ward, Ludlow B., 9
Ward, William H., Sr., 37
Warner, Erotus, 31
Warren, Maggie, 34
Waterbury, Lewis, 41
Waters, Zimri, 17
Watkins, Charles C., 36
Watkins, John T., 36
Watkins, Selinda, 54
Watrous, Daniel, 27
Watson, Caroline, 44
Watson, Joseph C., 51
Watson, Sallie, 40
Watters, Ella, 52
Weaver, Harry, 39
Weaver, Hattie, 27
Webster, Betsey, 9
Webster, John G., 42
Weeks, E. W., 14
Weet, Laura, 13
Welch, Kitty, 39
Welcher, Abigail, 15
Welcher, Byron R., 15
Welcher, J. P., 15
Wells, A. E. (Mrs), 45

Wells, C., 37
Wells, Emma, 37
Wells, Howland P., 26
Wentworth, A. H., 48
West, James W., 26
West, Solomon, 38
Westfall, Alice, 27
Westfall, Dewitt, 21
Westfall, George A., 13
Westfall, John R., 13
Westfall, John J., 24
Westfall, Mary A., 13
Wheeler, Benjamin P., 28
Wheeler, Solomon H., 28
Whitbeck, Frank, 32
Whitbeck, Henry S., 26
White, Emily, 41
White, Mary A., 36
White, Milo, S., 18
White, Mr., 52
White, Sarah E., 41
White, W. M., 47
Whitlock, Benjamin, 35
Whitlock, Levi, 35
Whitlock, Nelson, 34
Whitlock, Sarah, 34
Whitlock, Stephen E., 34
Whitney, L., 7
Whitney, Laura Louisa, 33
Whitney, Leon, 33
Whitney, Lottie, 33
Whitney, Mary, 7
Whitney, Mary E., 32
Wickham, Michael, 10
Wicks, Simon, 5
Wigglesworth, Albert W., 44
Wigglesworth, Mathew, 44
Wilbur, Andrew, 10, 33
Wilbur, Betsey, 10
Wilbur, Charles, 22
Wilcox, Eliza, 16
Wilcox, Flora E., 45
Wilder, John, 47
Willett, Josie, 20
Williams, Allen, 37
Williams, Amy, 9
Williams, Caroline M., 49
Williams, Charles, 13
Williams, Fletcher, 47
Williams, Frank E. (Mrs), 42
Williams, Hattie, 13
Williams, Helen P., 45

Williams, Joseph, 9
Williams, Richard S., 45
Williams, W. B., 44
Williams, W. H., 15
Willig, Rose, 42
Willson, Diantha D., 52
Willworth, Anna M., 14
Wilson, Isaac, 10
Winter, Charles, 38
Wixon, George, 51
Wolff, Ward, 6
Wolrath, George H., 38
Wolson, W., 25
Wolvin, Harriet, 52
Wood, Benham S., 35
Wood, Cornelia, 27
Wood, Edward A., 35
Wood, Ella, 54
Wood, Elmore, 16
Wood, John, 16
Wood, Nathan L., 33
Wood, Olive, 33
Wood, S. Therissa, 35
Wood, William, 41
Wright, George, 5
Wright, William B., 29
Wykoff, Charles D., 47
Yeo, Ella, 50
Yeo, Frank, 17
Yeo, John, 50
Yoemans, Mr., 27
York, Thomas, 31
Young, J. R., 51
Youngs, Alma Hendee, 38
Zimmerman, Ida, 30

www.ingramcontent.com/pod-product-compliance
Lightning Source LLC
LaVergne TN
LVHW051709080426
835511LV00017B/2823